Weird Parenting Wins

HILLARY FRANK

Weird Parenting Wins

Bathtub Dining, Family **Screams**, and Other **Hacks** from the Parenting **Trenches**

A TarcherPerigee Book

An imprint of Penguin Random House LLC
penguinrandomhouse.com

Illustrations by Hillary Frank

TarcherPerigee with tp colophon is a registered trademark of Penguin Random House LLC.

Most TarcherPerigee books are available at special quantity discounts for bulk purchase for sales promotions, premiums, fund-raising, and educational needs. Special books or book excerpts also can be created to fit specific needs. For details, write: SpecialMarkets@penguinrandomhouse.com.

ISBN 9780143132554
ebook ISBN: 9780525504474

Printed in the United States of America
10 9 8 7 6 5 4 3 2 1

Book design by Katy Riegel

For Jonathan and Sasha,

who make me feel like I'm winning . . .

even when I'm just being weird

Contents

Introduction

NINE YEARS AGO, during the last storm of the snowiest winter in Philadelphia history, my stomach began to gurgle loudly like a draining bathtub. It took about an hour to realize what this meant: my daughter finally wanted out.

Toward the end of my pregnancy, I'd discovered that my baby was facing my belly in my womb—"sunny side up," the midwives called it, which sounded to me like an apartment listing that calls a tiny studio "cozy." I was told to hang out on my hands and knees as much as possible and the baby should turn in time for delivery. She was angled in a way that meant she'd have to do nearly a full 360. Apparently fetuses can only rotate in one direction, like a flushing toilet.

I killed time in my last few weeks by watching the winter Olympics on my hands and knees. When I needed a break, I crammed—rereading key passages from my stack of childbirth books and handouts from classes at the hospital. Which breathing techniques to use for which stage of labor, which types of massage to request, which props to use. I was prepared.

Here is what I knew. If you just relax enough and surround yourself with people you trust, you'll be able to have a natural childbirth and it might even be euphoric; you must, must, must breastfeed the baby immediately after she is born, plus keep her in your room with you that first night no matter how tired you are; and, as detailed in *The Happiest Baby on the Block*, with Dr. Harvey Karp's five S's—swaddling, side/stomach position, shushing, swinging, and sucking—a bawling infant is magically soothed.

Here is what the books didn't tell me. That I would be in so much pain I wouldn't even want to be touched, let alone ask for a back rub. That the only type of breathing I'd possibly be able to muster was to blow raspberries. That I would get stalled for half a day at five centimeters. That just the teensiest, eensiest bit of Pitocin would send me into a series of ten-minute-long contractions that would leave me yelling for an epidural. That my baby wouldn't turn, making it impossible for me to push her out without an episiotomy. That she'd take her first poop inside me, breathe it into her lungs, and need to be rushed to the NICU immediately after being born. No nursing her; no keeping her with me in my room. I was kept up all night by a screaming newborn, but it was my roommate's, not mine.

They had Sasha hooked up to machines for the first three days of her life. I tried nursing her a bit, but we couldn't really seem to get the hang of it, especially with all those wires in the way. I was given a breast pump without much instruction, so I basically didn't use it. Besides, the only things holding me together were the moments that I could go to the NICU and put Sasha inside my hospital gown, pressing her warm bare skin against my own. I wasn't about to give that up to pump little splutterings of a substance that wasn't even milk yet out of my boobs.

A few days after we took Sasha home, we discovered that my episiotomy stitches had busted and I needed to be recut and restitched. It was sort of like going to the dentist and getting shot with local anesthesia, except in a much more sensitive part of your body. The surgery left me unable to climb stairs for two months—or walk, really—so I lived on an air mattress in my dark living room during that time. I couldn't stand long enough to change the baby's diapers. I couldn't carry her around to comfort her. I couldn't even sit and comfort her because sitting on my butt hurt too much. With the help of pillows and rolled-up swaddling blankets to get us in exactly the right position, I could nurse her. But it turned out that because I had neglected to pump at the hospital, I had low milk supply and had to feed her three ways each time she ate: at the breast, then a bottle of pumped milk, followed by a bottle of formula. I was swollen; I was sore. I wept every time I went to the bathroom, during every infrequent shower I took. There were fluids pouring out of me from every orifice, except maybe my ears.

We tried the five S's. We tried really hard. Sometimes they worked. But more often they didn't. And at those times we didn't just have a crying baby on our hands, we had a crying family. That's when we discovered the sixth S: shit out of luck. It all came to a head one night when my husband, Jonathan, was sick—passed out on the couch with a fever. It was 2:00 a.m. I was trying to nurse Sasha and she was yanking her head back and doing what Jonathan called her Fay Wray scream. She was clearly starving, but she just wouldn't eat. I frantically dug through my breastfeeding handouts, trying to find an answer. Nothing. It was too late to call anyone. I started doing this thing that I think a lot of people do when they're desperate, where I'd loop my memories over and over in my head. I'd relive the birth as if it were a movie and I'd always get stuck on this one frame. This split second during labor when I was sure, absolutely convinced, that if I had just gotten on my hands and knees one last time and accepted a massage from my midwife instead of opting for drugs, everything would have gone differently. I would've been able to turn the baby, which would mean I wouldn't have needed an episiotomy, which would mean I wouldn't have needed to be re-stitched, which would mean I'd be more capable with Sasha, which would mean she'd be happier right now, which would mean she'd be nursing calmly in my arms, gulping and making little sighs of baby satisfaction. But I was weak and I did choose the drugs, and here we were: Fay Wray. I was suddenly so full of rage that I nearly threw the baby across the room. It was the scariest thing I've ever felt, and I quickly put her in her bassinet and walked away.

When I told my friend Kirsten about what I was going through, about how I couldn't stop looping, she told me this: These first few months are the longest shortest time. Remember that. They seem like they'll go on forever. And then they're over. It's finite.

Now, nine years later, I know that parenthood is a series of longest shortest times. One after another. And I know that how-to parenting books are just suggestions. You take what works, leave what doesn't. Sometimes you are shit out of luck, and you just have to accept your shit-out-of-luckness until it passes. In the beginning, though, I naively assumed those prescriptive books held the answers. The magical, nonexistent answers to all things baby. And when those answers didn't work, I felt like I must be doing it wrong.

That's how most parenting books are written. It's my way or the highway. In our darkest hours, we cling to their authoritative words. And if they work, yay. We're winning at parenting. If not, we are lost. Even worse, we're bombarded with the authors' followers confirming our greatest fears: that we just became parents, and we have already failed. At one of the most vulnerable times in our lives, we're made to feel as if we're supposed to take sides in something as ridiculously named as the "Mommy Wars."

My kid goes to sleep on her own now. She's been doing it for years. And the things that worked did not come from books or experts. They came from friends, and experimenting, and dumb luck. When she was a baby, I learned that if I stroked the little curve above Sasha's nose, she was a goner. When she was a little older, I'd drive around town until she passed out, then park under a shady tree—and I'd lean my seat back and try to catch some Z's, too. These days, the thing that works best is an outright lie.

"I'll check on you in ten minutes," I tell her.

She looks at her clock and calculates. "Come at 8:47," she says.

"I will," I assure her.

We both know I won't.

The truth is, as we get to know our kids, we figure out what makes them tick. It's not going to be the same for me and you. Of course it isn't. We have different life experiences, different belief systems, different kids. But I guarantee you we've got something in common. The most effective tools we use to raise our kids—they're weird. They are often born out of desperation. They come from those rare times when, instead of freaking out—or, maybe, in *spite* of freaking out—we have a mad stroke of genius.

In this book, you'll find all sorts of strategies that real parents use—but would never be in a how-to style parenting book. Actually, "strategy" is maybe too strong of a word. Many of these wins were born out of trial and error; many are spur-of-the-moment white lies; some began as what seemed like parenting fails but somehow, impossibly, turned into moments of wonder or connection or mutual maniacal laughter.

Maybe someone else's weird parenting win will work for you, or will inspire you to try something new the next time you're stuck in a parenting rut. Or maybe some of these will just make you giggle when you can't remember the last time you did that.

The word "parent" in this book is meant loosely. We don't mean it in the biological, or even legal, sense. We mean any caregiver. Anyone experienced in creatively communicating with children. When we asked for people to send us their weird parenting wins, we heard from aunts and uncles, babysitters and friends. And if you've spent time around kids, you know that the intense challenges don't end in babyhood or little-kidhood. They just get more complex over time. That's why we included some mind-blowing wins from parents of teens, and strategies for managing relationships with grown kids. We collected ideas from all over the country—many internationally, too!—and the names in the entries are all real. I did, however, change some names in my personal essays to protect the privacy of the people in those stories.

At the end of the book you'll also find some weird kid wins. Because kids, of course, eventually discover they can manipulate us. Just like we did with our parents. I'm all too aware that it's only a matter of time before my kid is completely outsmarting me in this department. She'll be bragging to her friends about how she completely pulled one over on me, just like I brag now about my wins to my friends.

And, y'know, that'll mean I did it right.

Chapter 1

The Art of Soothing a Screaming Child

On fussy infants and toddler freak-outs—at home, in stores, and on the road

LAST WINTER, I took my daughter skiing for the first time. I am the kind of skier whose stopping method is a fancy maneuver I like to call Falling Over on Purpose. Still, it seemed like a fun way to spend a Sunday. The thing is, we hadn't realized the day before Martin Luther King Jr. Day is the busiest of ski season. We wound up waiting for skis for hours.

The weather was not on our side, and I didn't blame Sasha for complaining about it. She was cold, I was cold, everyone in line was cold. But after a while, her whining started grating on me and I worried that it was getting on other people's nerves, too. At first I told her that I heard her—I knew it was freezing. But all we could do was hop around, wiggle our limbs, hug each other. Anything to stay as warm as possible. She cycled through those things quickly and ended with a prolonged "I'm booored." Well, I was, too.

I started thinking, *How can I make whining more fun?*

"If you're gonna whine," I told her, "you've gotta sing the blues."

She grabbed my arm and hung from it with all her weight, groaning at my suggestion.

"*Duh-nuh-nuh-nuh,*" I sang, determined to make this work. She dragged me around in a circle by the hand, kicking at pebbles. But I kept going:

I was standin' outside
Waitin' on skis
Freezin' my butt off
Someone help me, please!
I've got the freezing-my-butt-off blues.

At the word "butt," Sasha lit up. Giggled. She loves the word "butt" so much. In fact, she's decided to *always* use that spelling, even when she knows it should be "but." Because it's funnier, duh.

Anyway, she was hooked. "Again, Mommy," she said.

I sang another verse of the "Freezing-My-Butt-Off Blues," this time with a slight variation—something about how waiting's the worst . . . and when you're in line you wanna be first.

"Now me, Mommy," Sasha said. She chimed in with her own verse, which I'm sure didn't rhyme. But it didn't matter. She was well distracted from the situation at hand—the very situation she was singing about.

We traded off singing lyrics and *duh-nuh-nuh-nuhs*, laughing every time someone said "butt." It's one of my favorite, most memorable parenting experiences. And it lasted maybe fifteen minutes.

Yeah, that's about how long I could stave off the whining. The triumph was brief, but it was major. Not only had I figured out a way to transform misery into fun, but Sasha had learned a new musical form as well as a way to express her emotions creatively—and, perhaps most important, she was entertaining me.

Imaginative solutions, though, take energy. They take headspace. They take being well rested enough to recognize you should be using your imagination in the first place. When you're so sleep-deprived you can't even remember the last time you brushed your teeth, and another person starts screaming in your face, all you can think is *nooooo!* Just, no more. Stop. You don't have the patience to take one more step and think, *How can I make this situation more fun?*

In my early days of motherhood, that's certainly where I was at. I wanted Sasha's cries to magically stop. I mean, if I could soothe her, great. That was the warmest, fuzziest maternal feeling in the world. But when I was spinning my wheels and the screaming kept going, I was left with *nooooo!*

You can't slip creativity into *nooooo!*

Remember that moment I told you about, when nothing would calm my kid and I felt a terrifying urge to throw her? It's no wonder I felt that way. Studies show that infant cries are effective because they motivate a parent to act. To keep this helpless being alive. But in some extreme cases, those cries backfire and spark such intensely negative emotions that they can trigger abuse. Chronic sleep deprivation also causes us to have a better recollection of distressing memories than happy ones. Sleep deprivation plus baby cries equals a dangerous cocktail.

Clearly, as a species, we need peace. We need quiet. We need moments to shut our eyes. To concentrate on what we're doing.

To reflect on what the hell has happened to our lives. To pass out. And that is why we desperately need some wins to soothe our kids. Because hopefully those wins will soothe us, too.

Once things started to normalize for me a bit, and I was able to sleep for four or five hours in a row, my creativity started coming back and I was able to work some sorcery into getting my kid to calm down. A lot of my wins happened in the car, which was a necessity because screaming plus driving is yet another dangerous cocktail.

Before my daughter could talk, I used to battle her car-screams by getting her to . . . well, scream. Just a different kind of scream.

See, I used to play this one song a lot. "I Want to Hold Your Hand" by the Beatles, but the Al Green cover version. In the bridge, I'd sing along with Al on the "I get highs"—and then after the last one, he lets out one of his signature high-pitched *aaaah*s. Those I'd leave to Sasha. The song lasts only a couple of minutes, so I'd put it on repeat and Sasha wouldn't have to wait long for her next scream. We once did this the entire way from our house in New Jersey to my parents' in Connecticut. In traffic.

It's a testament to how good that song is that I still like it.

When Sasha got a little older and was just starting to say words, I used a similar technique to keep her from falling asleep in the car. Car-sleeping on short trips was bad news because it meant she wouldn't nap at home. And those naps. Those naps were precious. They only went for twenty minutes, and I lived for them.

At the time, Sasha's favorite book was *Bear Snores On* by Karma Wilson. It's about this hibernating bear who snores and snores while his friends throw the party of a lifetime in his den. Of course, they wear themselves ragged. The story ends like this:

When the sun peeks up
on a crisp clear dawn,
Bear can't sleep . . .
But his friends snore on.

That little "on" at the end there—oh, that little "on." It was my best friend. Sasha was in one of those rear-facing car seats, so I couldn't tell if she was asleep unless I heard her. One day, as a test, I started reciting *Bear Snores On*. I slowed down at the end—but his friends snore—and I left off the last word. Miraculously, from behind me, came a scratchy-voiced "on." I did it again, and so did she.

On, on . . . zzzz.

Well, most of the time it worked.

Fussy Infants

When my older daughter was a newborn, she had some very cranky evenings. We had heard that white noise helps quiet screaming babies. We lived in a condo and so were conscious of how much noise our baby (and our white noise solutions) made—especially in the middle of the night.

During one particularly loud crying spell one night, in a moment of desperation, my husband grabbed his electric toothbrush and turned it on. He started waving the toothbrush around like a half-asleep orchestra conductor. And what do you know . . . the baby stopped crying! In a state of sleep-deprived euphoria, we took the head off the toothbrush and nestled the contraption next to our swaddled newborn. She—and we—drifted off to sleep. But an hour later, the toothbrush ran out of batteries and the screaming began anew.

We swapped my husband's toothbrush out for mine. And so began the nightly rotation of toothbrushes. While one was charging, the other one was somewhere within twelve inches of our beautiful baby girl. This was our new parent "make-it-work" strategy for about three weeks.

Did it work for our second daughter a few years later? Not a chance. **—Sarah, River Forest, IL**

When my daughter was between one and three months old, she was notoriously difficult to place down to sleep in her bassinet. She wanted to be held and cuddled while sleeping, and always seemed to startle herself awake as soon as she touched the mattress. We tried everything to gently set her down . . . holding our breath and praying that she wouldn't immediately start crying.

The win: We found that if I took off my pajama top and laid the shirt in the bassinet before placing the baby down, she would peacefully stay asleep. It was warm and smelled like mama—exactly what she wanted! I would simply put another shirt on and go back to sleep. Then repeat the whole thing in a couple of hours when she woke to nurse.

—Christine, West Islip, NY

After two kids, I think the key to managing colic is to think of what your child experienced in utero and try to match it. For example, with my first, I was a ballroom dancer before I became pregnant. I danced until almost full-term, so the rumba worked for him. With my second, I swam during my pregnancy, so placing him on my forearm and walking in a swinging motion worked—must have felt like swimming from his perspective.

—Kim, Washington, DC

Like many moms, I had a screamer. I was terrified to go anywhere more than a quick car ride away with her, never knowing when she'd unleash. At home, I knew that running the vacuum worked like *magic* to quiet her down—but in the car, I was lost. Then one day I tried tuning the radio to just pure static and turning it up moderately loud. It drove me bonkers but was certainly more bearable than the crying.

—Kerry, Charlotte, NC

Pathetic shushing never worked, but my husband discovered what he calls the race car song. Rather than shushing, he makes race car noises like an engine revving, and that calms my son down fairly consistently. I think the buzz of the sound is more soothing than the shushing, especially when done in close proximity.

—Sarah, Lincoln, NE

After hearing that the whir of the dishwasher had soothed a friend's baby, we tried it ourselves. Didn't work for us, but we went through all the kitchen appliances till we found something that worked. Turns out, our daughter was powerless against the white noise of the fan above the oven. She could go from full-on screamfest to completely asleep in less than a minute. —JORDAN, GLEN RIDGE, NJ

My grandma taught me to "buzz" to help babies sleep. She was a foster mom for a very long time to a lot of different babies. Needless to say, I trust her judgment. So I rock my four-month-old while doing my best bee impression, and he goes right to sleep! —NIKOLE, OREM, UT

On a couple particularly long nights, we'd put my now three-year-old in his Rock 'n Play in our pitch-black bathroom with the fan on and a constant recorded loop of us singing "You Are My Sunshine." —CASEY, FINDLAY, OH

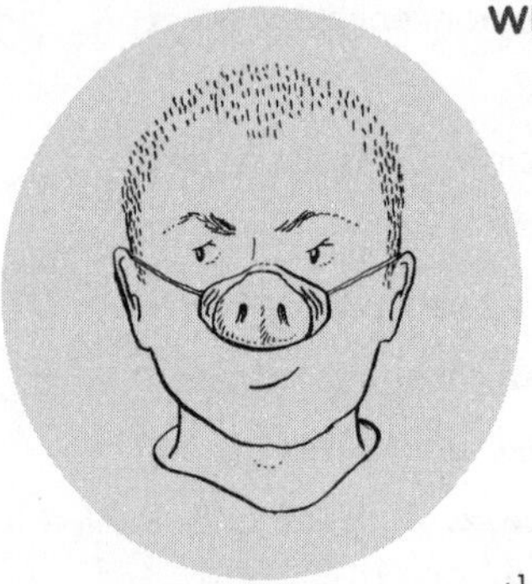

When our daughter was about three weeks old and crying all night, my husband found that if he made a really loud snorting sound, like an obnoxious pig, close to her head, she would instantly stop crying, at least for a moment. It seemed like a primal reflex: "I have to be quiet now because there is a big weird something right there." Sometimes, in that moment, she could start to settle down, sometimes not. We would only repeat it a couple of times. If it did not work, we would admit defeat and go on to something else. Who knows what our neighbors thought!

—Allana, Montreal, QC, Canada

My son only took naps in motion with background noise playing loudly. During those days, I would place a portable speaker in his stroller and roam around the streets of Philadelphia with jazz blaring. I figured jazz was a genre that would not be offensive to fellow pedestrians. (Can you imagine if I blared heavy metal from our stroller?) It ended up feeling quite pretentious, like we were walking around to an old-timey theme song, announcing our arrival. Not only did our "jazz walks" calm my son and allow him to nap, it was amusing to watch all the passersby look around bewildered, wondering where the jazz music was coming from. **—Aimee, Philadelphia, PA**

Colicky infant win: walking in circles with my son singing TV theme songs. His favorites were *Growing Pains, Fresh Prince of Bell Air,* and *Perfect Strangers*. I didn't even know I remembered the words to those songs, but it was all I could think of in the moment. **—Molly, Bellingham, MA**

My daughter (now fabulous) was an incredibly fussy infant. The only thing that kept her from crying was bouncing with her on an exercise ball while listening to the hair dryer on high, all while singing "99 Bottles of Beer on the Wall" to keep my sanity. **—Becca, Minneapolis, MN**

When my two-year-old daughter fights bedtime, my husband and I put her in her crib and do a synchronized dance to a Delta Spirit song. The fussing usually stops when I pop out from between my husband's legs for the "ooohs."

—**Kari, Vancouver, WA**

My daughter is adopted and she is biologically my niece. Still with me? So I always think of my sister growing up (her biological mother) when I'm faced with how to handle situations with her. My daughter went through a phase where she wasn't falling asleep well at night. She would cry for up to two hours (of course I was in and out of the room the whole time) before she fell asleep. I tried different things, including playing soft music. My daughter *loves* music. Nothing worked.

Finally, one night, I thought back to my sister always *blaring* dance music from her room at all hours of the night. Her music would blast through the entire house and keep us awake while she snoozed soundly. I decided to try it. The first night, I played Justin Bieber through the speaker on her baby monitor. She fell asleep within ten minutes. That sealed the deal. My husband went out the next day and bought her a wireless speaker, and every night we blast Justin Bieber, Katy Perry, Lady Gaga, Twenty-One Pilots, and more to put our two-year-old to sleep. The type of music and the volume at which it is played in her room is what makes this so strange to me. But hey . . . whatever works!

—**Lisa, Smyrna, DE**

When my daughter was an infant she hated the car, but she'd stop crying if I sang "I'm Henry the Eighth, I Am" in a high-pitched voice.

—**Clair, Philadelphia, PA**

Surprising Songs That Have Soothed Real Babies

"Rollout" by Ludacris

Opening theme to *The Sopranos*

"Juicy" by the Notorious B.I.G.

"You Shook Me All Night Long" by AC/DC

"Moonage Daydream" by David Bowie

"Let's Get Loud" by Jennifer Lopez

Opening theme to *The Golden Girls*

"The Origin of Love" from *Hedwig and the Angry Inch*

"Get Your Freak On" by Missy Elliott

"O Canada"

"Folsom Prison Blues" by Johnny Cash

"Wake Me Up Before You Go-Go" by Wham!

"Cherry Pie" by Warrant

"Jump in the Line (Shake, Señora)" by Harry Belafonte

Car Freak-Outs

Our little guy *hated* riding in the car—would scream the whole time we were driving anywhere, near or far. Tuvan throat singing was our go-to music to help calm him down, but during one trip we forgot to bring along our Huun-Huur-Tu CD (disaster!). In sheer desperation, we ended up teaching ourselves how to do Tuvan throat singing over the course of that hour-long drive! I never got very good at it, but my husband can now throat sing simple melodies like "Baa, Baa, Black Sheep." For about a year, it was one of the few things that could keep our kids happy in the car. **—Sarah, Ottawa, ON, Canada**

My youngest, Charles, *hated* car rides with a fiery passion. He had the staying power to make every drive, from two minutes to two hours, absolute torture. One day, running out of songs to sing, I randomly mimicked the sound of those long annoying car alarms and he stopped crying. From then on, I would sing the car-alarm song whenever we were in the car. My husband even recorded me singing it on his iPhone as a memo so we could play it over the speaker and save my voice.

—Dani, San Diego, CA

I use the Bluetooth lady in my car to calm my screaming six-month-old. I just keep saying "help" and she keeps repeating the same thing over and over—sometimes I even have her read my phone book till my daughter falls asleep. My two-year-old son can now recite all my contacts, but tends to pronounce them wrong due to how the computer simulator does.

—Kassandra, Crooks, SD

My six-month-old doesn't like car rides and cries a lot in the car. I've tried singing, talking, different music, white noise, driving with the windows down. Nothing has worked. Well, today it was just her and me on the commute home from work. We were stuck in rush-hour traffic and she started crying. It occurred to me to bark like a dog—and it worked! She stopped crying. But as soon as I stopped barking, she would cry again. So today, I barked like a dog all the way home. Woof woof!

—Rachel, Brentwood, CA

We turned our car's hazard-light button into an "eject" button! It worked like a charm to snap our young son out of any tantrum he was having during a car ride. His imagination took over and he would start imagining the sunroof opening up, his seat becoming airborne and landing with a parachute on the sidewalk. It's not our proudest moment as parents, but it snapped him out of it! **—Mia, New Rochelle, NY**

On a road trip through the Black Hills I taught my fourteen-month-old how to play the kazoo. I had picked one up for free somewhere and it ended up in the diaper bag. When she was starting to lose it, I pulled out the kazoo and it kept her entertained for a good ten minutes. It was loud and annoying but better than crying! **—Hilary, St. Paul, MN**

How have I gotten my kid to stop freaking out in the car? Clanking a wedding ring on a metal water bottle. Somehow the jarring noise gets her to stop crying, at least momentarily.
—Michelle, Providence, RI

Separation Anxiety

My daughter cried every time I dropped her off at preschool. It was a big change for her, and even though she recovered quickly after I left and enjoyed her time there, she cried and clung and protested. Each day, it tore my heart out and I worried what the teachers thought of me—I might look like I was ignoring her, or if I paid attention, I might look like I was enabling her. This had to stop. I wanted her to be more independent. When I dropped her off next, she put on the face that told me she was getting ready to cry. I put it to her as a choice she was making: "Do you want a happy goodbye or a sad goodbye?" She's the kind of person who will dig in and commit to her choices, so when she said "sad goodbye," I figured it had backfired.

But then I realized that improv comedy could save me. The golden rule of improv is to say "yes, and." That is, to agree with my daughter, and then heighten it. So I told her she would indeed get a sad goodbye. But I offered: "How about I'm the one who's sad, and you have to tell me to leave?" The power reversal, as well as the comedy potential, were immediately attractive to her.

For weeks after that, she gleefully asked for sad goodbyes, and while I pretended to cry and cling to her, she would protest, "No, Daddy, no! Go!" While she pushed my legs toward the door and I pleaded and reached for her, the other kids watched us, mystified, and Noa emerged triumphant, job done, with no tears.

—Ari, Chicago, IL

My daughter's daycare in New York City had this ingenious trick at drop-off time. The parents didn't "leave"—instead, the children pushed us out the door.

We've carried this with us through the transition to new classrooms, new schools, and even new cities. We've done it with sitters, grandparents, playdates, you name it.

—Megan, Dallas, TX

My four-year-old likes Star Wars, specifically Darth Vader. He also has a hard time with drop-off at school. To get him excited about my departure, he waits by the gate as I slowly drive past with all my windows down, blasting the Darth Vader theme song. This happens daily between 9:00 and 9:30 a.m. with my son and about six other preschoolers cheering me on.

—Kimberly, La Cañada Flintridge, CA

My son is three years old and recently changed rooms in his daycare. Say goodbye to toddlers and diapers, and say hello to preschoolers and tiny, tiny urinals. This switch threw him for a loop, and drop-off anxiety sky-rocketed.

This daycare has a wall of windows that looks out toward the parking spaces. Thus, our new routine was born! I take Declan to his room, tell him a story, a secret, and then I promise my "funny dance." He slowly detaches from my leg and runs to the window to watch the spectacle. I typically throw in some running man, robot, and booty-shaking from the parking lot—but sometimes I break out the moonwalk. Then he's laughing and ready to go back to the classroom area and play. I even get random applause from passersby on occasion.

—Alison, Elmwood Park, IL

A week before my daughter started childcare, I slept with a lovey (small blanket with an animal head) so that it would smell like me. It worked wonders to calm her down, and months later it is still a comfort to her even though I'm sure it has lost my scent. **—Cassie, Aubrey, TX**

When my naval officer husband was deployed for twenty-one months, I made a Flat Daddy to attend special events and keep the kids company when they missed him. We took the Flat Daddy with us to performances and propped him up when we were hanging out. **—Erin, Where the Navy Sends Us**

My wife and I have five-year-old twins who started kindergarten this year. Kindergarten brings big change, and for my kids that big change was taking the bus to school. On day one, my kids emphatically displayed that they hated the bus. They cried and screamed, and my wife and I literally had to push them up the bus steps. My kids then dragged themselves down the bus aisle and found a window seat so we could continue to see them crying.

The bus would generally sit and wait for the traffic light to change. So I decided to use the time to cheer my kids up. I would blow them kisses or fake-cry, then wave at them and chase after the bus for at least a block. My kids were so perplexed by my behavior, they'd stop crying as the bus pulled away.

As the weeks passed, I became obsessed with getting them to smile on the bus. I kept trying to top myself—running into street lamps and doing balance-beam acts on the ledge around the tree in front of their bus window. Once I even climbed the tree! That's when the other kids on the bus took notice of me.

After that, everyone looked forward to my "act." All the kids would enthusiastically wave at me as I chased after the bus.

Now my kids love the bus and they don't even look out the window to see what I'm doing anymore. Sadly, though, I'm still up to my antics. I can't figure out how to top climbing the tree, so I just repeat my act. I should confess, I'm a professional comedian—I need the attention. Hopefully someone is watching. **—John, Brooklyn, NY**

Toddler Tantrums

Instead of buying our four-and-a-half-year-old daughter lots of commercialized dolls of characters she wants to play with, we go online and let her choose a stock image of the character (Elsa from *Frozen*, for instance), print it out on thick paper stock, cover it in package tape, and cut it out. She then has her own homemade, fairly durable paper doll of sorts. She has dozens of these now, which she plays elaborate pretend games with. The characters come from movies, books, shows, and even real life. For example, she has Beyoncé, Hillary Clinton, and Alexander Hamilton (as portrayed by Lin-Manuel Miranda) dolls. We call them "printouts." Our daughter doesn't mind that they're two-dimensional and it saves us a ton of money! **—Julia, New Haven, CT**

This is a win of my mom's that she used often when my sister and I were kids. After getting sick of hearing us beg her to take us to Toys R Us, she told us that Toys R Us was like Costco; you needed a membership to get in. Since we didn't have a membership, we weren't allowed to go. We accepted this as truth and never asked her again! Her cover was blown later when our babysitter took us to Toys R Us and looked confused when we asked about her membership. **—Jamie, Sacramento, CA**

When I first started taking my son shopping and he would get a little bored, I'd play Crazy Driver with our shopping cart. I'd race through an empty aisle at top speed, swerving side to side like mad, saying, "Crazy Driver! Ahhhhh!" If there was someone in the aisle, I would pretend we were still crazy but hiding the fun from other shoppers. And as soon as we were in the next empty space, we'd go "crazy" again. I love that he picked up on this pretty quickly, too—like together we were pulling one over on the world. As he grows older, this is expanding into our life in general. When a task isn't pleasant but needs to get done, he knows we can act like giant goofballs together to help push through it. **—Cassandra, Rochester, MN**

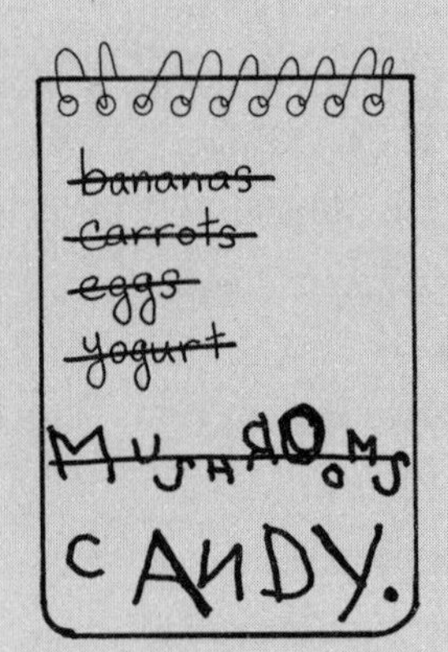

My oldest son, Max, had a notepad that he could draw in while we shopped. As he got older, he started managing my shopping list for me. He would ask what word on the list matched an item we picked up, and it was his job to cross it off. As he got older, he wrote the list for me. He always stayed engaged and usually didn't fuss about going shopping. I think this was because he felt important and needed to do a job. He also chastised me if I picked something up that wasn't on the list. I remember he insisted on writing mushrooms because they weren't on the list, just so he could cross them out. He couldn't have been older than four or five. **—Trisha, Rockford, IL**

When my kids were old enough to be mobile at the grocery store, the checkout "gauntlet" was always a challenge. All the candies were eye level to them, brightly colored and within reach! In order to avoid a screaming fit, and to be able to get checked through quickly, I made a matching game out of the situation. Every candy bar that was in the wrong place got picked up and placed with all its "friends" in the correct spot. This approach satisfied the kids' urge to touch the colorfully wrapped candy, and they enjoyed putting them in the right place. This continued well through their elementary years. At checkout time, I was able to tend to business, while they quietly straightened up the candy displays!

—Pamela, LaPorte, IN

When my toddlers scream "no," I pretend to hear them as saying the name "Mo."

I say: "Mo? Who's Mo? I don't see any Mo. Where's Mo?"

More often than not, it goes from tantrum to giggles in a few seconds. **—Aaron, Chapel Hill, NC**

One day, in the middle of my oldest daughter's tantrum, my sleep-deprived, caffeine-addicted brain cells concocted an idea! She was around five years old and obsessed with a mood ring her grandma had given her. I sprinted in my out-of-shape way to my room, grabbed the ring, and huffed back to her. Showing her the ring slowed her down a bit, and in that moment, I slipped the ring on her finger and reminded her of the colors and their meanings.

After she saw her own mood color, I cautiously suggested that she focus on reaching the calmer and happier colors. She loved the idea and was so busy channeling her energy that she forgot about her terrible, horrible, no good, very bad mood.

Who knew the cheap little mood rings I devalued in my youth would one day save my sanity? **—Tandra, Mebane, NC**

I learned early on that the words "secret" or "special" could have a magical effect. If my daughter was threatening a tantrum over having to leave the library, I could promise her an exit through "the secret staircase" (the back stairs). The mystique of the "secret" was just enough distraction.

This, however, backfired when we visited a small, quiet church. During Communion, she caught sight of the wafers and bellowed for a "SPECIAL COOKIE!"—much to the amusement of the congregation. **—Anne, Shelburne Falls, MA**

When my son was two, he was obsessed with candles for a little while. He was just starting to be aware of things like holidays and birthdays and would wander around my parents' house finding all their candles and asking to be able to light them and then blow them out. One day, around that time, he got super frustrated about something, the way toddlers do—it was probably cereal in the wrong-color bowl or something—and I knew that some deep breaths would help him cool down a little, but toddlers do not always understand breathing. It suddenly occurred to me to help him out with his favorite activity. I held up three of my fingers and told him they were candles and asked if he could blow them out. It still takes some modeling, and sometimes I make the candles a little resistant to extinguishing until his breaths are really getting longer and slower. Since then, it's turned out to be an effective strategy for other parents we know, and his younger sister now walks over and asks to blow out candles when she's feeling upset and overwhelmed. **—Cheryl, Atlanta, GA**

I tell my daughter to take a deep breath by breathing in through her nose and out her mouth. I tell her to try to "blow me away." When she breathes out, I run or fall backwards dramatically. **—Meghan, San Luis Obispo, CA**

My usually mild-mannered kiddo was having an absolute meltdown. We had tried everything to get him to calm down with no success. Suddenly I reached down and pulled his shirt right over his head. I don't know where the impulse came from, but it surprised everyone so soundly that it resulted in giggles and a nice quiet night after. **—Alejandra, Davison, MI**

My daughter has perfected the art of the epic tantrum. Sometimes what works is to say, "I'm going to make you into a pizza!" And then I pretend she's the dough and roll her out, spread sauce and cheese, throw some pepperoni on there, and put her in the oven. I've also made her into pancakes or cupcakes. If it's the right approach for the moment, she usually ends up laughing and smiling and wants to do this over and over.

—Vanessa, Glover, VT

When our kid is in a fit on the ground, my husband picks up our dog, hovers him over our daughter, and the dog will give her kisses until she starts laughing. This usually works, and sometimes it makes her mad that it worked. Either way, the fit is halted. —HANNAH, SAN DIEGO, CA

I noticed that when my daughter got sleepy or upset, she would search out one of my bras and hold it up to her face and kind of snuggle it; eventually a light bulb went on and I cut one up for her to sleep with . . . just the cups. They are basically her version of a blankie. I tried to call them her snuggles, but my four-year-old couldn't help but throw in the word "boob," so they have been dubbed her "boob snuggles."

—SHANNON, MOUNT HOOD, OR

Whenever our toddler falls down or runs into something, my husband and I immediately start cheering and clapping. He looks up at us, smiles, and goes back to playing. His teachers tell us that when his friends fall, he starts cheering and clapping, and then they smile and go back to playing. This has stopped many tears, and I like to think this gives him confidence to know that when you fall down, you can get back up smiling, ready to try again. —MARISA, NASHVILLE, TN

On our local hiking trail one day, we saw a girl who was maybe five or six with her face absolutely covered in red lipstick. Like, the Joker style, *allll* around her mouth. And as she traipsed along behind her parents, she just kept reapplying in a big circle, content as could be.

"Looking good!" my husband said, encouragingly and with a thumbs-up. "She's allowed to wear as much lipstick as she wants when she hikes," the mom explained. I mentally filed that one under "For Later Use."

—**Casey, West Kill, NY**

When my son was about five years old, we moved home after having lived abroad his whole life. He would have hysterical tantrums that he just could not pull himself out of. One time when he was inconsolable, I did a yoga headstand in the middle of the living room. He'd never seen anything like it! Another time we were in the shopping center, and I turned on my heel and started walking backwards. I told him I was a world-champion backwards walker and he'd probably be pretty good at it, too, since he was my kid. Worked for me! —**Elanor, Sydney, Australia**

When my son was three, the seizures that he was having interestingly gave birth to an intense and unexplainable love for numbers. He searched for them all over, wherever he could find them: numbers on the TV remote, the oven, a calculator; numbers on apartment doors, on elevators, and on the street signs as we walked from block to block. His favorite number searches would happen in taxicabs, where we would play a game and look for the numbers one through ten—not just in the taxi ID, but any numbers on the doors, the tiny TV screen, and even the cabdriver's license.

What was especially unusual was that his language was very much delayed, except with numbers. Not only could he recognize them, but he could also name them verbally well beyond twenty. When I would come home from work each day, instead of greeting me with hello, he would say, "Number one!" and I would respond, "Number two!" which translated to "Hi, Mommy!" and my response of "Hi, Boo-Boo!"

This presented a great challenge for his speech therapist, who was working very hard on developing his oral language. She discouraged us from relying too much on numbers when he could be using typical words and phrases. We tried very hard to limit number talk and foster language, but sometimes we just couldn't help ourselves. Whenever he cried, all we had to do was scribble down some numbers on any available piece of paper and hand it to him. He would immediately stop crying and begin admiring his good friends, numbers one through twenty. His diaper bag quickly became a trove of loose, wrinkly receipts, take-out menus, and backs of envelopes with increasingly larger grids of numbers. The routine bought us time we selfishly wanted to finish the food shopping, take longer walks, and linger at coffee with friends. The jig was up, though, the day I reached into my bag to give something to his speech therapist and papers full of numbers spilled onto the floor between us like contraband.

My son is seventeen now and has plenty of language, and his love for numbers is not what it once was (coincidentally, his seizures have been controlled for years). Knowing that we did not damage him for life, we can now share with pride the parenting hack we once discovered!

—Jennifer, Westport, CT

Chapter 2

The Art of Getting Your Kid to Eat Stuff

Food trickery for babies and picky eaters

BACK WHEN I was in preschool, I thought eating was a waste of time. Why eat when you could be dialing your plastic rotary phone, pretending to call the boy from your playgroup who didn't know your name? Or running up and down the hallway of your apartment in Underoos? Even fake-cooking at a play stove my mom had rescued from the street trash was more fun than eating real food.

And so my mom invented chicken snack.

Chicken snack was not a meal; it was a snack. I mean, obviously; just look at its name. Never mind that my mom had breaded a chicken cutlet, seasoned it, and baked it in the oven—along with the other chicken cutlets she and my dad were going to have later that night. Chicken snack was cold. It was cut into cubes. And you ate it with a toothpick. On a stool by the kitchen sink. Not at the dining room table.

See? *Snack*. Not boring old dinner.

Okay, okay, yes. I'd been had. Not to mention I was a big dummy for hating food.

Of course, now, as a mother myself, I get why my mom had tricked me. Kids need nutrients. How would I have mustered the energy to call the boy who didn't know my name without a protein boost?

I hear lots of parents fretting over whether their kids are ingesting enough of the right stuff. Calcium, iron. And, ahem, vegetables. It's likely that the average American child's abhorrence to veggies is largely cultural—plenty of children around the world regularly consume veggies fuss-free. I mean, some food aversions are genuine for sure. But kids also relish a classic battle of wills and toddlers quickly learn that their parents care a lot about what goes in their mouth. Lots of kids go through phases, too, or change their minds about the foods they like. My daughter used to love avocado; now she'll only eat it if it's presented as guacamole. And chicken kebabs used to be her favorite dinner—until that day when she asked me if this was the dead body of a chicken in her mouth. Which was the last time she ate meat. Except for bacon. And salami.

Sasha has always liked beans, so I haven't been too worried about her protein intake. And she likes certain veggies, but I also want to make sure that my young self-proclaimed vegetarian eats more than bell pepper strips and carrots sliced in circles. Lettuce, for example, has been a challenge. And I have to say, I can't blame her. Lettuce is limp. It's blah. Especially if you haven't developed a taste for salad dressing.

One day, though, I accidentally stumbled upon a solution to my lettuce problem.

Have you ever seen the very first SNL Digital Short? It aired in

December 2005 and it's called "Lettuce." The video is presented as a PSA from the United Lettuce Growers Association. In it, a forlorn Andy Samberg and Will Forte sit on a brownstone stoop, commiserating over the loss of a friend—all the while pausing to take bites out of a head of iceberg lettuce. Like, mammothly huge chomps. One day I showed Sasha the video, thinking she might get a kick out of it.

And oh, did she ever.

She loved it so much, she demanded that the next time I went to the grocery store I buy a head of lettuce. She specified that it would be *her* lettuce. Not mine or Daddy's. She kept bugging me about it, asking if it was on my shopping list.

When I finally came home with the lettuce, Sasha couldn't wait for me to put away the groceries; she dug around in the bags until she found the lettuce, then begged me to get my phone and shoot a video of her. We unwrapped the lettuce, stood her by the wall, and I started rolling. She actually did a pretty good Andy Samberg impression. Like, lettuce-eating-wise. And ever since then, lettuce has been a regular part of her diet. Not just iceberg either.

Sometimes I think that food, when it comes to kids, is all about context. Snacks trump dinner; chomping lettuce from a handheld ball trumps gingerly nibbling it from a plate. Even when Sasha was nursing, context was key. When I held her to my breast, she'd refuse to latch even though she was clearly hungry. My pal Kirsten watched this happen while she was visiting—the same Kirsten who gave me the name for my podcast.

I remember tearfully saying, "See? I can't do it. I can't get it right."

Kirsten was like, "Hang on, can we try something?"

She took Sasha out of my arms and repositioned her so that

she was sitting up beside me on the couch, facing my chest. She was too young to be able to sit up on her own yet, so Kirsten propped her up with a pillow.

"There," she said. "Now try."

I don't know why, but this angle worked. Sasha latched right away. Maybe it was a reflux thing? All I know is, they taught me a bunch of different positions in my breastfeeding class, including something they called the "football hold." But what I really needed was the prop-your-infant-up-as-if-sitting-in-a-chair hold.

As Sasha grew, it was clear she was super social. Even as a baby, she always wanted to be a part of the action. And at holiday meals with family, she far preferred being held to being in a high chair. But holding her wasn't the safest idea if, say, your bowl was full of scalding hot soup—a conundrum that my husband cleverly solved by placing Sasha on his shoulders. He'd hold her there with one hand while slurping soup with the other. That move did backfire one Chanukah when, unbeknownst to us, Sasha was brewing a virus . . . and threw up on his head. Just prior to that, she'd gotten her first taste of Grammy's homemade chicken soup, carefully blown upon till it was cool enough for a baby tongue. Sasha instantly opened her mouth for more. It was clearly her favorite thing she'd ever tasted.

Until a few years later, when she found out it was made of dead chickens.

Feeding Babies

I got a *lot* of clogged ducts when I first started nursing my son. I could feel those suckers in there, but no matter how much I massaged, I never quite managed to work them free . . . until I tried a waterproof vibrator plus steaming hot shower. MIRACULOUS. My husband was mortified to have company over because there was always a neon blue vibrator hanging out somewhere in the bathroom, but I was well beyond caring. **—Tessa, Berkeley, CA**

At three months old, my baby, Alvin, has started paying more attention to his surroundings. During bottle-feeding, he often refuses to eat more after one to two ounces and starts looking around. My pediatrician suggested that I bottle-feed in a dark room with no sound and no TV, but Alvin just refuses to cooperate.

My father, who is currently staying with us in the same house, invented a trick: He sucks the bottom of the bottle while telling the baby that he is also enjoying the milk—you'd better finish yours before I drink it all up! Alvin finishes drinking in just seconds! **—Fangfang, Mountainview, CA**

When I was a newborn, I would fall asleep while nursing and not get enough to eat. My dad would keep me awake and nursing by putting ice cubes on my feet!

—Elizabeth, Brooklyn, NY

I helped my son night-wean by putting Christmas lights on a timer. I told him that whenever the lights were on, he could nurse, and when the lights went off, nursies would be asleep. When I wanted to nurse more, like because he wasn't feeling well, I just kept the lights on, and when I felt touched out, I turned the lights off quicker. He was twenty-three months, so he was ready for weaning, and this worked really well. **—Jana, Portland, OR**

My nine-month-old baby wasn't interested in foods offered to her; yet she acted as a human vacuum cleaner, readily eating anything she found on the floor. So I put some food on the floor. Bits of rice cakes and other foods, and it worked. She ate them! **—Kate, Lyons, CO**

When my baby was transitioning to solid foods, she absolutely *refused* to be spoon-fed. It was incredibly frustrating, and I was always anxious that she wasn't getting enough to eat. She would get so angry and throw everything on the floor at almost every meal. Then one day when she was around thirteen months, my husband and I decided to go out to eat at a sushi restaurant and bring her along, and we inadvertently figured out that if we offered her food from a pair of chopsticks, she would very happily taste almost anything (and actually eat a bunch of it, too). I am still not sure *why* this technique works—it could be because the chopsticks are less invasive in her field of vision, or maybe she just thinks they're cool? But it *works* and now we keep the diaper bag and kitchen stocked with chopsticks at all times. At twenty months, she is still fascinated by them and is even learning to use them herself—although we have to watch her so she won't poke her eye out! **—Anna, Newburyport, MA**

White Lies for Picky Eaters

When my brother and I were little and would go out to eat, my parents would allow us to have one soft drink each, and once that was done it was only water. One day, my four-year-old brother was making such a fuss about not wanting to drink water that my mum told him it was special "Pepsi water," as it had been served in a glass with the Pepsi logo on the side. He happily drank it down, and from that day on, he claimed he only liked "Pepsi water." For ages after, my mum would refill a Pepsi bottle with tap water to get him to drink water at home.

—Sophie, Edinburgh, Scotland

I've been a single working mother from the start but have always tried to feed my son nutritious meals. He's turning eighteen soon and has still never eaten from a fast-food restaurant.

As he got older I fed him some variation of my own meals in smaller, less spicy portions. For a while, he became a pickier eater around preschool. He began turning up his nose at too many of the foods I put in front of him. It was frustrating and bewildering.

Thankfully he has always enjoyed Thai, Vietnamese, and Chinese food. My weird parenting win was inspired by one of our meals out. When I unloaded our leftovers at home one night, I realized there was an extra empty container. I stored it out of sight for later use. Then another night, after I put the kiddo to bed, I loaded up the unused take-out container with homemade leftovers. After work the next day I said, "Hey, guess what—we have takeout for dinner!" He clapped his hands with glee and ate his meal without complaint. I purchased extra containers at a restaurant-supply store and hid them out of sight at home. For a few years I employed that subterfuge, but only once a week or so. And I quietly retired the trick before he ever caught on. **—Sharyn, Minneapolis, MN**

When I was a toddler, I was an extremely picky eater. The one thing I would eat enthusiastically? McDonald's Happy Meals. Both of my parents worked full-time, so I was often fed by a nanny who indulged my fast-food habit, likely exhausted by the prospect of trying to get me to eat anything else. My mother devised a genius plan to trick me into eating greens, fruit, and meat that had not been breaded and fried. She went to McDonald's and asked if she could take some empty bags, cups, and napkins. She then placed all of my meals inside McDonald's-branded packaging. Steamed string beans? McDonald's makes those now! Tuna fish sandwiches on wheat bread? That's part of the newest Happy Meal! By the time I was wise enough to catch on to her scheme, I had developed a palate for more than fries and chicken nuggets (but I still like those, too!). **—Rebecca, Brooklyn, NY**

When our daughters were around three and six years old, they decided that they no longer liked pork chops and only liked chicken. I took pork chops off the menu for a couple of months, and one day we had a new dish called French Chicken. They enjoyed this new dish, and it was several years until they figured it out.

—Charleen, Texas

My two-and-a-half-year-old son thinks pumpernickel toast is chocolate. The other day he had a tea egg (traditional Chinese snack) and asked if this was a chocolate egg. I told him it was. **—Jessica, Acton, MA**

My five-year-old would not eat my mashed potatoes—granted, they were instant. My husband would use the same measurements out of the same box and my daughter would eat them, couldn't get enough. But if I did it, she wouldn't touch them.

So I started calling them "hot ice cream," and she devoured them. We would have Chicken Fried Steak with Hot Ice Cream. She couldn't wait for dinner. **—Lily, Fort Worth, TX**

Lies About the Ice Cream Truck

- It's the music truck.
- It's the dancing truck.
- It only plays music when it's out of ice cream.
- It's bad, old ice cream. The stuff in our fridge is fresher.
- It's the fish truck. All those kids running toward it? They just really, really like halibut.

Cultivating Adventurous (and Healthy) Taste Buds

Cutting strips of frozen spinach off those blocks you get from the grocery store freezer section turns an unpleasant vegetable into a tasty frozen treat for my toddler. No joke, I easily get her to eat just plain spinach this way on a regular basis. I don't even want to eat just plain spinach! **—Stacen, Stow, MA**

I just got my three-year-old to eat beets by telling her that if she eats them, tomorrow she might have pink poop! After laughing hysterically, she said that will be "so beautiful and so yucky!" And then she proceeded to eat them all!

—**Carolyn, Brussels, Belgium**

My eight-year-old son is a really, really picky eater. He's also got an eagle eye for veggies or other nutritious sneakiness hidden in his food. So sometimes I put spinach in the marinara sauce or a little bit of avocado in his hummus, and then we have "fancy dinner." I will announce that it's a fancy dinner night. We get out the good china and fancy crystal goblets, we sit in the dining room, and most important, we turn off all the lights and eat by candlelight. Which, by the way, makes it much harder for him to see all the tiny details of his food. —**Jillian, Knoxville, TN**

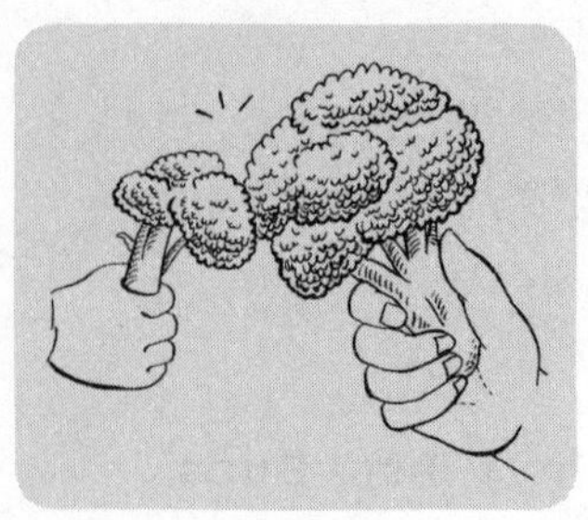

I get my fourteen-month-old daughter to eat more by toasting our food (the cheers kind of toast, not the toaster kind). One night my husband and I were having wine with dinner and we clinked our glasses together. My daughter held out her piece of broccoli for us to toast her, and I did, which she thought was hilarious! Now she does it all the time, which I don't mind, because after we clink our food together and say cheers, we both have to take a bite.

—**Amy, Vancouver, BC, Canada**

My husband doesn't allow our daughters to eat vegetables. He says they will become too strong and they will win if they play a game we call Boxing. Boxing is lying on the floor, feet against your opponent's feet, trying to throw them to the side.

Our daughters are three and five, and during dinner, they frequently ask their dad to turn around to look at the bookcase. Then they gesture to me that they want more vegetables. When he turns around, they laugh and say, "We are eating vegetables! We are eating vegetables!" He playfully pretends that he is angry and they laugh even more. It's been working for years now.

—Anouk, Bremen, Germany

My oldest is the pickiest eater. He has promised to become a veggie eater when he turns five (the clock is ticking).

One night we had raw carrots as our veggie, which his little sister happily munches. I declared that we would have a "crunch contest," with the loudest crunch winning dessert. I awarded points with each crunch. After one round, my son actually asked for a second carrot so he could crunch louder (cue my jaw hitting the floor). **—Megan, Phoenixville, PA**

I filled a PEZ dispenser with frozen peas. My two-year-old devoured them, luckily before they thawed.

—Diane, Berlin, CT

Being vegetable farmers, we are always keen to see something green on the plate. Our children, however, always seem to gravitate toward carbs, particularly roast potato wedges. We used to grow zucchini, which we refer to as baby marrows. The marrows would be steamed and cut into slices, making round discs. We would then serve these with whatever main dish, and the children could "buy" some potato wedges by eating some "marrow money." **—Ian, Malelane, South Africa**

"Birthday cereal" is huge in our family. My mom started it. During the week of our birthday, we got to pick *any* cereal we wanted at the grocery store (think Lucky Charms) and eat it until it was gone. It felt so indulgent that we looked forward to it even more than our cake, and we never complained about only having healthier cereal options the rest of the year. **—Becca, Minneapolis, MN**

My *very* strong-willed then-kindergartener was refusing foods in such a random way that it became obvious it was about control. Things he used to like were suddenly disgusting, and no new foods would be eaten. I was doing everything I could, cooking foods I know he'd eat, trying to stand my ground, but he was so skinny already . . . finally I resorted to this.

I sat him down and told him he could have one dinner veto per week. If he vetoed, he could have a peanut butter sandwich, no questions asked. But if he used his veto, he had to eat whatever we had on the other nights of the week without any substitutions. *But,* if he didn't use any veto that week, he got a golden ticket, and four golden tickets was worth a trip to the movies.

I swear to you, he never used a single veto. At first he considered it every night, asking what we were having the next night, weighing his options, and then giving in and eating what was in front of him. I always made sure that dinner was something a reasonable kid would try, and he did! We did a few months of it, saw a couple of movies, and eventually it just petered out. Now, at nine, he eats pretty much whatever we give him.

—Mary, Victoria, BC, Canada

To get our toddler to drink anything, we pour the drink into a tiny medicine cup and call it "tiny milk." We have to refill it every few minutes and it definitely makes me feel like a bartender, but it gets her to stay hydrated! **—Tim, Seattle, WA**

When my wife wasn't home, I used to cook fish sticks for me and my kids. Problem was, they hated fish sticks and we would sit at the table for hours while they would cry and whine about not wanting to eat the sticks. So I started baking an odd number of sticks and I told my two kids, "Whoever finishes their fish sticks first doesn't have to eat this last stick." My kids ate so fast, and I think my daughter might even like fish sticks now!

—Paul, Tuscaloosa, AL

Our favorite way to get our two-year-old to eat all the things on his plate is to give him control. First, my husband, my son, and I all grab our forks. Then we take turns picking what we are going to eat. Naturally, my son, Everett, always picks rice or a potato. But he picks for *all* of us. So it's "Okay . . . potato! Get ready [potato on all our forks], get set! GO!" When it's his turn, he gets to pick what we eat, and he gets to say, "READY! SET! GO!" and we all eat it. What he hasn't figured out is that when it's my turn or my husband's, we always pick the meat or veggies. We like to get creative and sometimes draw out the "Readdddy . . . set . . . . GO!" And sometimes we whisper it. So far we are on three weeks of solid full-plate eating. **—Michelle, Yardley, PA**

Our daughter has never been a big fan of typical American kid food or kid menus. When she was three, she went from eating spicy foods, hummus by the spoonful, and Indian and Thai food to being a very picky eater. Luckily, this only lasted a few months, but in that time I realized that anything they were sampling at Costco was interesting to her. So I started playing Costco Sample Lady with her at mealtimes. I'd put various foods on a plate with toothpicks stuck in them, or serve messier foods in little plastic containers, and she'd gobble everything right up.

Now, at nine, her favorite foods are lamb saag, curries, and pho. **—Laurel, Cottonwood Heights, UT**

My wife and I are of mixed heritage: I'm Chinese; she's Finnish, Norwegian, and English. We've tried very hard to preserve both cultures in everything from the food we eat to what is considered polite at our table. Long story short, we now have a five-year-old daughter who eats a balanced diet and loves vegetables and whole grains. On her second birthday, we asked her what she wanted to eat. Without any prompting whatsoever, she picked chicken feet and tripe. It was, and still is, a pretty proud moment for me. **—Jeremy, Calgary, AB, Canada**

Our middle daughter was a really picky eater for a while. My husband came up with this strategy: She loves the limelight, and he agreed to film her on his phone talking about how much she loves certain foods, like peas. She immediately started trying all kinds of new foods, just to be filmed.

About two years later we got worried about the kids being skeptical of global foods. We started making foods from other countries and learned that they were totally down for trying them if we hyped the country enough. The biggest hit was playing the country's anthem (thanks, Wikipedia!) before dinner starts, but they also love looking at pictures of the country and learning fun facts about it. **—Sarah, Evansville, IN**

My husband and I received a stuffed bear head as a gift from a very strange uncle. We do not hunt, but we thought it would be hilarious to put it up on the wall in our dining room. This all took place pre-baby. Fast-forward to our sweet, petite one-year-old. You just never know when the little toddler lady-child is going to eat what we give her. So as a form of mealtime ritual, and a way of getting her pumped up to eat, we salute the bear. Sounds crazy, but we all say, "Hi, bear," and wave at the bear head. She loves it. We look forward to the day that she asks why other kids do not salute the bear.

—Genevieve, Minneapolis, MN

One thing I have been doing with my sons, seven and nine, for the past few years is Dinner in Odd Places. I do it on nights when things seem to be a bit off, or we are just needing an energy boost. After dinner is prepared, I shout, "Dinner in odd places!" Eyes widen and you can see the wheels begin to turn in their small heads. We then begin to brainstorm places we can eat: hallways, under the table, in the garage, bathtub, closets, in the bunkbed, the car. It helps to shift the day a bit, and the spontaneity often leads to deep connection.

The weather is beginning to cool here in Texas, and we have already named our next location. Pizza on the roof.

—Mark, San Antonio, TX

I've found that if they're hesitant about eating something or flat-out refuse to try something new, just say, "It'll make you fart." They'll dig into it with this "What a fool I was!" look on their face. **—Erin, Petal, MS**

I got my kids to eat chickpeas by calling them butt beans. "This butt bean is pooping in my mouth!"

—Kristin, Charlottesville, VA

The place where my kids went to preschool had a snack served to the kids. Sometimes it was something unusual or different for someone. They would make a big deal, bring out special hats, and pound on a drum and announce, "Connor is going to take an 'adventure bite' of . . . cottage cheese." There would be an accompanying drumroll, and celebration would ensue after adventure-bite success. A certificate would go home, too. We adopted this strategy at home (with slightly less fanfare) and still use it today with my four preteens/teenagers. **—Beth, Seattle, WA**

Growing up, my parents had a wonderful trick to make us eat our yogurt. We would not just have yogurt; my brother, sister, and I would have firemen's yogurt.

We would wear real firemen's helmets and eat yogurt that my dad would pour into our bowls while standing on top of a stepladder. He would even try to pour from as high as he could without spilling the yogurt. If we were really lucky, we could sit on the stepladder and eat our yogurt there.

—MARGOT, UTRECHT, THE NETHERLANDS

Chapter 3

The Art of Getting Your Kid to Act Like a Person

On getting out the door, bathing and grooming, potty stuff, manners, cleaning up, and going to bed and staying there

WHEN SASHA WAS about a year and a half, we bought a potty. A little red plastic one, which we placed on the bathroom floor beside the regular toilet. I'd have her sit on it before her bath—and lo and behold, sometimes when she'd stand up there would be pee in the pot.

This is gonna be easy, I thought.

I was too new to motherhood to realize that exhibiting smugness is the parental equivalent of answering the phone in a horror movie. Forget it, you're doomed.

Just weeks after introducing Sasha to the potty, she broke her leg. It happened on a crisp fall day at the playground. She was standing at the top of a slide, looking like she was about to run straight down it, so I climbed the ladder in a flash, superhero-style, to save her. I grabbed her, put her on my lap, and away we flew. Down, down, down. On the way, the rubber sole of her shoe nicked the side rim and I heard one of the most horrible sounds of my life: the snap of her tiny tibia. I learned later at the hospital that this kind of injury is so common in young kids that it's known as a "toddler fracture." And it often happens when kids ride down slides on a grown-up's lap. Parenting PSA of the day: No lap-sliding with toddlers.

After the broken leg, everything came to a screeching halt. My previously sleep-trained child reverted to crying all night long. She wouldn't go anywhere without her pacifier. Preferably one in her mouth *and* one in her pocket. And potty-training? Well, forget the potty; I was lucky if she'd poop at all. This is when I learned the phrase "poop withholding." I loaded her up with pear juice and pouches of mashed prunes. Still, she withheld for nearly a week.

Sasha's cast stayed on for two months. When it came off, I thought it might be a good time to start trying the potty again. And she seemed mildly interested in the red hunk of plastic sitting in our bathroom. By that I mean, she'd treat it like a relaxing piece of furniture. And it's just rude to poop on nice furniture, right?

Then came the bathtub incident.

One fateful night, I was giving Sasha a bath. She was splashing around, singing, obsessively pouring water from a cup into the narrow spout of a toy boat. Suddenly a look came over her face, like, *What is happening?*

Poop. Poop was happening.

This thing—it was the size of her entire arm. And when Sasha turned around and saw it, she screamed as if she'd actually lost her arm. I pulled her out, toweled her off, and held her in her rocking chair while my husband went on poop duty—which I hear was not an easy cleanup job.

This poop. It 100 percent destroyed Sasha.

I tried to tell her it wasn't a big deal; we all poop in the tub sometimes. Over the next few days, I called relatives, getting them to tell stories about how they'd pooped in the tub when they were kids. Maybe that was true, maybe not—but they went with it. I took out every poop book at the library I could find. One made poop seem normal, another scientific, another funny, another cute. Sasha listened to the books with indifference. She would not poop. It was back to Withholdingsville, this time for a much longer stay. Maybe it's a local custom in Withholdingsville for residents to not bathe? Because Sasha wouldn't do that either.

We tried all kinds of things. New toys! Bubbles! Bath crayons! *Are you kidding me? You don't want to draw on the walls?!* I even stripped down and got in the tub myself, inviting her to join me. Which, in retrospect, was maybe more of a turnoff than an incentive?

Anyway, none of it worked, and when she got extra stinky, we would just stand her on the bathmat and sponge her down. For a couple of weeks she didn't get shampooed. Or maybe there was a splattery attempt over the sink? It's all a blur.

Now, seven years later, I have a kid who runs her own bath. She showers from start to finish by herself. How did we get here? So simply, it's embarrassing to think we didn't try it sooner. One night after coming home from work, my husband filled the tub a few inches. He stood Sasha on the bathmat, looked her in the eye, and calmly but firmly said, "You're going in."

She said no, swung her arms around, stomped up a storm. But he just picked her up, lowered her in slowly, and hugged her while she tantrummed. He kept holding her, telling her she was fine.

And after a few minutes . . . she was. Later that week, bath time had become her favorite part of the day.

The poop thing was a bigger challenge. How do you slowly but gently force someone to move their bowels? A person can drive themselves crazy asking that question. Trust me, I am one of those people.

I wish I could tell you exactly how we found our way out of Withholdingsville. But I'm afraid I'm not exactly sure what route we took. Plus, we were in a car being driven by a two-year-old.

In the end, I think it was just a matter of Sasha pooping in her diaper a few times and realizing she wasn't gonna poop out a limb. I remember a couple of times cheering her on while she braced herself on the nearest vertical object—a kitchen stool, the neighbor's front steps—knowing that her purple shaking face meant she was finally letting it go. (That's what that *Frozen* song is about, right?) I realize that one day Sasha will read this and hate me. Baby, I just want you to know that everyone has pooped in their pants while grasping a kitchen stool. We'll call all of our relatives, and I promise, they'll agree.

Well, great. Sasha was pooping. But now we had to get it to land in the potty. By now, all of her pals were doing it. Lining up to use the pint-size toilets at daycare.

Nothing that worked for them seemed to work for her. Not setting a timer, not toilet-time reading, not a sticker chart, not any of the various seat inserts I'd borrowed from friends, not running around pantsless. Lots of people swore by that one, saying kids feel embarrassed when they pee on the floor or the couch. Sasha did both of those things, and neither one seemed to bother her in the least.

I wanted to not worry about it, just let her tell me when she was ready. I wanted to be that kind of laid-back mom. But I also think there comes a time when you just want your kid to step up and do what you know they're capable of, whether it's using the toilet or brushing their teeth or having table manners or getting out the door on time. I say this, fully recognizing that kids come with different capabilities and that we need to temper our expectations with reality. But I knew Sasha was capable of this potty thing; for some reason she just didn't want to do it. And what really made me nervous was, we were getting awfully close to her potty refusal actually having some real setbacks—just like, eventually, if you don't say "please" and "thank you," nobody will want to have you over for dinner. Or if you never learn good mouth hygiene, you'll have a rough time scoring a first kiss.

Sasha's third birthday was looming. Three is when society—at least American society—decides you're not a baby anymore.

You get to take drop-off classes, without an attending grown-up. You get to go to pre-K. And according to packaging, you can play with smaller toys because you're not gonna try and snack on them.

That last one Sasha had under control. The other two, though? Those were up for grabs.

At three, she'd be eligible for child-only swim classes. Which was pretty exciting because she loves the pool. But in order to attend, she had to be potty-trained. It makes sense; you don't want the teacher having to deal with your kid's mess. The thing is, Sasha had been taking classes with a friend who was the same age. Born just two days before Sasha, in fact. And the way it was looking, her friend was gonna advance but Sasha wouldn't. All because of this potty hang-up.

How do you tell a child who only comes to your waist, "Well, honey, you could be in that class with your friend, but they don't take kids in diapers"? Um, actually, in a moment of weakness I think I told her something pretty close.

At the same time, I was enrolling Sasha in pre-K. I really liked this school; it was super diverse. Plus, there was a bilingual program, which I thought would be a great way for Sasha to connect with my husband's parents, who are both Latin American immigrants.

"Oh, yes," I told the nice lady taking my paperwork. "She's definitely potty-trained." If it turned out she wasn't, it would be a deal-breaker.

In reality, Sasha had recently peed all over a friend's beautiful hardwood floor immediately upon being dropped off for a playdate. That, following an attempt to see what would happen if I just straight-up put her in underpants.

Well, Sasha did wind up getting to go to that school. And that swim class. All because of one thing: a calendar.

I went out and bought a cheap little calendar from Muji. I told Sasha it was hers. And I asked her to mark a day in January that would be the Last Day of Diapers. We also picked one to be the Last Day of Pacifiers. She circled one day for each and I wrote in the words.

Somehow, though, I don't think Sasha quite understood what she was signing up for when she circled those dates. When we tried to take away her prized possessions, she freaked. So much for proclamations of "last days."

But, my friends, a birthday can be a powerful thing. And Sasha's was just a few weeks away. We revised our deadlines, circling her birthday for giving up diapers; a week later for pacis.

Well, on this kid's third birthday, she ran into our bedroom to wake us up. She told us she was ready. We grabbed her last box of diapers, ceremoniously sealed it up with packing tape, and marched it up to the attic—for her younger cousin, she said, as if they were just another hand-me-down. And that was it. She's been going in the toilet ever since. Amazingly, she didn't even need diapers at night. Which maybe shouldn't surprise me, given her proven withholding skills.

That birthday, Sasha also decided she was ready to go paci-free. No one-week waiting period needed. We'd been planning a big celebration where we'd tie a pacifier to a bunch of balloons and watch it sail away. (I was later told you actually need an absurd number of balloons to make this work.) But no, she wanted all pacifiers out of her face *now*. It reminded me of when my brother was a toddler and my mom somehow convinced him to throw his beloved bottles in the garbage and he gleefully pressed the button on the trash compactor. And now I am realizing that my brother will also hate me for writing this.

Sasha has no memory of her poop-drama days. In fact, one summer we were on vacation with my brother's family when he was going through a potty-training battle with his three-year-old daughter, Hana. That week, my brother and his wife had decided they were gonna try the bare-bottomed approach. Like Sasha, though, Hana had no qualms about peeing while playing.

Sasha, who was six at the time, looked at her, incredulous. "Why're you peeing on the *floor*, Hana?" she asked.

And Hana has been peeing in the toilet ever since.

Peer pressure to the rescue.

Getting Dressed and Out the Door

I had been a docent at an art museum for many years. My daughter grew up going to the museum and was used to getting a bit of special treatment when she visited. All of the guards knew her, and she liked using my key card to open the secret door from the galleries to go into the office area.

Back when my daughter was five years old, my wife was traveling when I was scheduled to give a gallery talk. That meant I had to take our daughter with me. We had to do that a few times in the past, and it always worked well. She was well behaved, and she stood next to me, holding my hand for the forty-five minutes it took to give the talk. People thought it was cute to have a kid standing with the docent.

But on this particular day, she really, really didn't want to go to the museum—tantrum-level not wanting to go to the museum. And then it hit me. We could do a project together to make her very own museum staff ID, which she could wear while we gave the talk together!

We sat down at the computer. We scanned my ID, and we took her photo. I opened Photoshop, and we pieced together an ID for her that was indistinguishable from mine except that her title was "Kindergarten Docent." We printed it on a good printer using high-quality paper. I had an extra ID sleeve and lanyard, so we put it in there and it looked perfect. She was thrilled—and ready to go give her gallery talk!

It was only then that it dawned on me what I had done. I had just taught my five-year-old daughter how to make a perfect fake ID! I'm hoping she doesn't remember that lesson when she reaches the age where she wants one for Friday nights. —Todd, New York, NY

I worked as a wildlife educator training and handling exotic animals before my eldest son was born. Now that he's four, he's *crazy* for animals and fiercely independent. I've taught him all about biology, ecology, animal behavior—and, yes, how to train animals using operant conditioning (positive reinforcement when an animal completes a desired behavior, with no punishment if they opt out).

My son loves Komodo dragons, mainly because he's impressed that they're *real dragons*. He's invented a whole Komodo personality for himself, complete with a name (Brillia) and backstory that he uses for imaginary play. Funny thing is, he's *waaay* more cooperative as a Komodo than as a human child, so whenever we're struggling to get through bath time, get ready for school, or any other time-sensitive, patience-sapping moment, I ask him to flip into "Komodo mode." Then he's eager to please and follow any "training" directive to be rewarded with an imaginary rat as a Komodo snack! —Amber, Clovis, CA

Our daughter is five, which means she doesn't always listen when we're talking. She's also a dreamer, which means she often quietly talks to herself, concocting imaginary stories and dialogue.

Requests like, "Sadie, please put on your shoes, we're running late to school," inevitably turn into, "SADIE, GET YOUR SHOES ON NOW! THIS IS RIDICULOUS, OTHERWISE NO TELEVISION FOR THE REST OF YOUR LIFE!"

That doesn't work out very well for anyone.

So we've recently replaced long phrases with clearly stated nouns that cut through the noise. When she needs to put on her shoes, it's simply: "Shoes. Shoes. Shoes. Shoes." Dinnertime and she needs to go and sit at the table? "Food. Food. Food. Food."

A single word often breaks through her cloud of thoughts and dreams and procrastination and actually gets heard by her little ears. **—Matt, Philadelphia, PA**

Beginning at about two and a half, my daughter decided to dawdle when getting dressed in the mornings. She also complained about getting dressed after bath time. I asked myself, *Why am I insistent on her wearing playclothes and pj's when, essentially, the clothes are the same—that is, soft, stretchy knit material for both shirts and pants?*

Light bulb moment: After bath time, help kiddo get dressed into playclothes. Skip pajamas all together. To make this technique work, you must be sure that (1) only seasonally appropriate clothing is available for the child to choose from and (2) the adult has to let go of any stress regarding mismatched clothing (stripes plus plaid or dinosaurs plus polka dots).

—Beth, Silver Spring, MD

I play "Flight of the Bumblebee" on my phone. The song inspires both my little boys, ages four and a half and two, to speed up their getting-dressed routine. They try to "beat the clock" and finish before the song is done.

—Clare, Minneapolis, MN

My son really, really hates getting dressed in the morning. It took me a long time to realize that this was partly because he hates putting on "cold clothes." He now gets dressed without a fuss . . . because I put his clothes in the microwave for fifteen seconds first. Toasty warm clothes are a lot more tempting! (Watch out for metal zippers though!)

—**Kjerstin, Madison, WI**

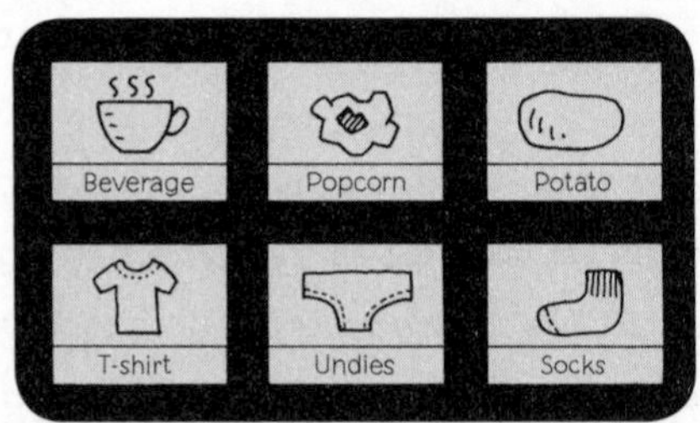

Getting dressed is an undesirable chore, but our kids—ages two and four—get a kick out of "surprising" us with their outfits. They both disappear into their rooms and come out dressed. This routine has eliminated the argument about getting dressed, although it has led to another issue: We have very little control over the outfit choice. My son's favorite choices include sweatpants and a T-shirt in exactly the same color (so they "match"), paired with his Mickey Mouse or Christmas bow tie. My daughter's crazy concoctions usually consist of multiple pairs of underwear, a dress with a tutu under it, and at least four large headbands. In her opinion, less is not more. But at least everyone is dressed, and no one is crying!

—**Lauren, Commerce, MI**

Despite my best efforts, my daughter dove into a princess phase for a few months one summer when she was two. Fall rolled around and it was getting chilly, but my daughter was insistent that princesses do not wear tights or leggings of any kind under their dresses. And all of this was without her ever having seen a Disney movie or knowing any of the princess characters, so I wasn't going to bring those up as a reference. Instead, I tossed the idea out on Facebook: Any older princesses out there that will video chat with my daughter and explain to her that princesses really do wear warm clothes in the winter? I found an old friend from high school who lived across the country and her daughter who agreed to the plot. They dressed up, and during a video chat they shared many words of wisdom about princesses: that they could wear coats and gloves and leggings when it's cold out; that they didn't even need to wear a dress to be a princess; and, of course, that princesses can do and be anything regardless of how they looked or dressed. My daughter didn't get frostbite all winter.

—Ariah, Minneapolis, MN

I was able to convince my three-year-old to wear a button-down shirt to church by telling him that it was the type of shirt Clark Kent wears over his Superman clothes.

—Melissa, Arlington, VA

My mother, a former registered children's nanny in Great Britain, has so many magnificent stories and techniques. One of my many favorites that she used to employ on me and my older brother, Tom, was to make us pretend to be robots!

She would program us with the task, usually along the lines of: "I'm going to program you to get ready to leave the house with all your things for school in five minutes." This was followed by Mum pushing the "buttons" on our back, whereupon we would go about the task and move in a robotic manner and speak in a robotic voice. "I am going to brush my teeth. I need to put my shoes on." **—Nick, Cardiff, Wales**

Teeth, Nails, and Boogers

My son has been struggling with his tooth-brushing routine. This past week, we've been pretending that a bird made a nest in his mouth. A blue bird with some pink and purple feathers. It's been laying eggs, and the eggs are hatching. We find the bird on Monday. On Tuesday, we clean out the nest; then we clean out the baby birds on Wednesday; then the twigs the rest of the week. He decidedly doesn't want a bird living in there. No birds, no eggs, no hatchlings, no twigs, no slugs, no spiders, no worms—he wants clean teeth!

—Olga, San Francisco, CA

We were struggling with getting our kids (two, three, and four) to willingly open their mouths for toothbrushing, until we realized that if we asked them to say "pee" and "poop" over and over, they would make the correct mouth shape for front brushing and devolve into maniacal laughter for back brushing.

—Amanda, Austin, TX

To get my four-and-a-half-year-old and three-year-old to open wide and brush their teeth, I taught them to sing the song from *The Little Mermaid*: "Ahhh-ahhh-ahhh . . . ahhh-ahhh-ahhh!"

—Crystal, London, ON, Canada

My two-year-old son is not a fan of brushing his teeth. My two-year-old son *is* a fan of trying to lick me. My parenting win: "If you brush your teeth, you can lick my face." It's pretty gross, but he is brushing his teeth and I smell minty fresh.

—Jane, Cape Town, South Africa

After my three-year-old saw *Annie* for the first time, she became kind of obsessed. So I started playing *Annie* with her at night while getting ready for bed. I'd be Miss Hannigan, and she'd be Annie. And I'd basically just bark orders at her to get her pajamas on, go potty, wash her hands, and brush her teeth. I simultaneously felt mean and like a genius for figuring this out (an evil genius mom, maybe?). But she loved it and thought it was the most fun game ever.

—Jen, New Brunswick, NJ

My son always hated having his nails cut. When he was eight or nine months old, we discovered (through a dramatic reading of Shel Silverstein's poem "Sick") that my husband could distract him and hold his attention with a very dramatic and drawn-out fake sneeze, allowing me to trim his nails. The fake sneeze became part of our regular routine until shortly after he turned one, when he wised up and we had to switch to an Elmo video.

—Elyssa, Kensington, MD

When my daughter was around eighteen months, she started to notice that sometimes the nail clipper didn't get all the way to the end of her nail and it would hang a bit. My husband or I would just give it a gentle pull to remove the nail. She thought that was the best thing ever and started asking (and now at three, demanding) to pull the last bit off herself. She loves to get her nails trimmed because of it!

—Rebecca, Jersey City, NJ

We (mostly my wife, really) made a game out of nail trimming. On walks to preschool in the stroller, whenever we pass a fire hydrant, our son gets to pick which finger or toe we trim. Double win, the game transferred to hair trims, too, which used to be a horrible fight. I don't claim that they're great haircuts, but it keeps it out of his eyes. —Kate, Chicago, IL

My three-year-old, Lucy, hates to have her nails trimmed. She will tolerate it only if we can save all the clippings in a tiny little pile so she can throw them away when we're done.

—Bethany, Nashville, TN

My five-year-old daughter and two-year-old son both hated having their nails trimmed. My win is to put them in chairs and sit on the floor (or deck if it is nice) and pretend we are at a spa. The five-year-old gets a pretend manicure, and then the toddler wants to do what his big sister is doing, so he goes second. It takes about five minutes to do both kids' finger- and toenails. —Jennifer, Dayton, OH

I still bite my two-and-a-half-year-old's nails. It's not weird yet . . . ? —Chelsea, Grand Rapids, MI

My daughter, like most babies, loathes having her nose wiped. She flails, beats her little fists in the air, and more to avoid the incoming towel.

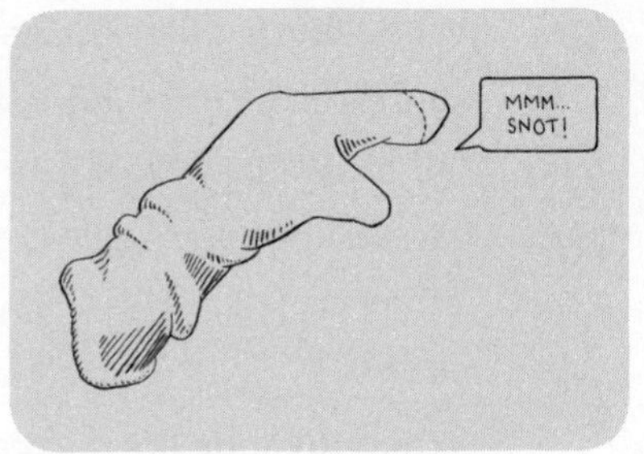

Unless . . . it's a sock. An old sock made to look like a Lamb Chop puppet—though no decorations needed. Just a sock on the hand with the pushed-in appearance of a yapping mouth. The sock talks to her, makes her giggle for a moment, and then "nibbles" her nose—as in, surreptitiously wipes the snot fountain clean. No complaints, no tears, no protests. And all those singleton socks lying around finally have a good purpose! **—Natalie, Pittsburgh, PA**

When I was a kid, my dad told me that since I seemed to like eating my boogers so much, he would start saving his own boogers to feed to me. Of course, he was kidding, but just the thought of it disgusted me so much, I never ate my boogers again! **—Jenn, Forestville, CA**

Bathing

My daughter was a foster kid. She came to us when she was two and a half. She is biracial and had a huge lion mane of thick curly hair. It was beautiful, when she would let me take care of it. Getting there was a struggle! She was terrified of water, to the point where she freaked out when she saw a waterfall in a park. So, as you can imagine, washing her hair was an ordeal! She would only let my husband wash her hair, and we had to get swimming goggles for her to wear when he did. She is seventeen now and has taken over her hair care herself. I'm happy to report that she is no longer terrified of water either. **—Mary, Springfield, MO**

When our toddler decides he doesn't want us to put lotion or sunscreen on him—inevitably when we're mid-application—we tell him, "Okay, we'll just rub it off," and proceed to act like we're doing so, effectively rubbing it in and finishing the job.

—Sydney, Denver, CO

When my kids are reluctant to get into the bath or shower, I can always entice them to quickly get in by telling them we're having a "painting party," which consists of letting them paint themselves and/or each other with soap squeezed onto clean paintbrushes. **—Nina, Los Angeles, CA**

My daughter was not super keen on taking her bath—*until* we hit on "techno-bath!" We bought some glow-stick bracelets in bulk, and we crack a couple of them, turn off the bathroom lights, and play music. They are really fun and look cool in the water. This also allows for moments of parental pride when my daughter, instead of asking for kid's music, requests Whitney Houston, Prince, or David Bowie! **—Dixie, Chicago, IL**

My husband is redoing the bathroom in our house that has a tub. The other just has a small square shower with a shallow basin and no ability to plug the water. My one-year-old and three-year-old do not like shower water falling on their heads. In order to give them a "bath" in the shower, I pull out our plastic disc sled, which fits perfectly in the shower, and I fill that with about two inches of water. **—Hillary, Lyndhurst, NJ**

I turn my toddler upside down to wash her hair. No soap or water in the eyes, and being upside down seems to be interesting enough to make the hair wash bearable. I stand in the bathtub with her legs around my waist, bend over to turn her upside down, and wet her hair with the hand sprayer. Then stand her up to shampoo, then turn her upside down again to rinse. **—Reanna, Joshua Tree, CA**

My son is really into chemistry or "making potions," as he calls it. We've mixed the Old Faithful geyser with vinegar and baking soda. Other concoctions are more run-of-the-mill four-year-old elixirs: a container filled with rocks and dirt or a bottle of paper towels, water, food coloring, and glue. But tonight, he really wanted to make a potion and I didn't have time. So I said I'd let him make a potion in the tub. He reluctantly agreed, and then I thought, "Oh, great. Now I'm in a sticky wicket. How am I going to get him clean in a potion bath?"

Well, the idea came to me just when I needed it. My son was sitting on the couch playing on his Kindle when I approached him with the ice bucket from the fridge. "It's time to make your bath potion," I said, and shook the ice tub. He looked up, excited. Was I really going to let him dump all of the ice into his bath? Oh, yes I was! Video game discarded, he happily marched down to the bathroom. As he poured the ice, he really enjoyed hearing the cracking sounds and the visual of ice instantly shrinking. The win for me? I had made the water in the tub too hot, and this was my instantaneous solution to get it to cool down while also fulfilling my promise of bath-time brew.

—Micah, Saint Louis, MO

My four-year-old has hated taking baths for months, especially with his two-year-old little brother. I froze toys into ice cubes and now he cannot wait to get into the bath because he likes to melt out his toys from the ice. And they take baths together! —JOY, SAN MATEO, CA

Pee and Poo

My son is almost twenty-one months old. And being a busy guy, he gets pretty upset about diaper changes. He screams, he kicks, he flips over—I think he's going to be a fabulous wrestler in high school.

The other day, as he started crying, I just started pulling diapers out of the package and throwing them at him. I put one on my head. I started asking him, "Here? What about here? Do they go here?" He started laughing. Then we played peek-a-boo with one on his head. So far, it's still working—the old diaper-to-the-face trick is pretty funny even after a few weeks. —EMILY, PORTLAND, OR

My husband discovered when our oldest son was about eight months old that we could keep his hands out of his poopy diaper during changes if we sang "TUMMY DRUM!" and got him to drum happily on his bare stomach over and over while we dealt with the mess. We have since successfully used this method with our younger twins and have passed it along to friends and family. I've never had to clean poop off of hands after changing diapers as a result.

—WENDY, ALTAMONT, NY

Both of my kids hated pooping in their diapers, and I hated cleaning poop that's been squished all over the place, so from early on we did elimination communication. That's when you hold a baby over a toilet, sink, or potty when they've just woken up or when they act like they need to go. Sort of like potty-training, minus the training, because babies do it instinctively. I'll admit, baby poop is kind of gross to wash down a bathroom sink, especially when you're out and about and it isn't *your* sink. But you get to have fun making faces at each other in the bathroom mirror, and the mirror helps me keep track of what happened potty-wise. The toilet avoids the gross factor but is pretty boring. You and baby are just sitting backwards on a toilet staring at the bottom of the toilet lid. Enter (drumroll) cut-and-stick mirrors! I bought a sheet on Amazon and cut it to fit the bottom of the toilet lid, with holes for the bumps that touch down on the toilet seat. My friends must think it's weird that I have a mirror on my toilet, but potty time is forever transformed.

—Anna, Seattle, WA

When my son was about eighteen months, he wore "monkey diapers" (Luvs-brand diapers with the monkey on the front). Well, I didn't know the monkeys were that important to him and I bought a few packs of Target's diapers that were on sale. He had a fit and kept ripping them off because they didn't have the monkeys on them. So I took a pen and drew a monkey on his diaper. It got to a point where I would sit down with a stack of diapers and a Sharpie and would draw monkey after monkey.

—Rachel, Perkasie, PA

When my toddler twins are having a tantrum (especially during a diaper change), I hand them a random safe object. Our favorite thing that usually snaps them right out of it is a small heavy-for-a-kid metal doorstop. It's so unlike their usual toys, they are fascinated by it! **—Jessi, Albuquerque, NM**

We had a bouncy chair that we deemed the "poop chair." We'd put her in it in just a diaper in the late afternoon (always the biggest blowout poo of the day). She'd poop in it and we'd just clean the liner. Beautiful stuff. **—Hanna, Golden, CO**

As my due date came close, other moms thought it was appropriate to tell me the horror stories of motherhood. One of the stories was public blowouts. I knew I could handle labor, sleep deprivation, and even toddler tantrums. But public blowouts became a huge fear of mine. The horror of poo getting everywhere and not being prepared to get my baby (or myself) cleaned up was awful. So before we checked out of the hospital after my little poop monster was born, my husband and I raided the room. We took a whole stack of those blue pads they put under you for bleeding and a box of gloves. Our diaper bag always has those, a change of clothes, and a resealable bag. If a blowout does happen, the strategy is gloves on, strip the kiddo over the blue pad, and clean him up. The pad, diaper, gloves, and even dirty clothes all get bagged and tossed.

This once saved us while touring open houses. The Realtor offered the couch so we could change our son's diaper. As soon as my husband got the diaper off, the projectile poop began.

We whipped out the pad and gloves, did the routine, and ran out of there. The couch was saved.

—Chelsey, East Windsor, NJ

When my baby has a huge diaper blowout, I put him in the dry bathtub and change the whole diaper in there to contain the mess. It's much easier to wipe poop out of the tub and do a quick tub clean rather than wash the change pad cover, the wall, the carpet, or anything else. I can also rinse out clothes or rinse off baby, as required. **—Emily, Edmonton, AB, Canada**

I'm now the mama of one diaper-wearing baby, but for years before motherhood I was a full-time nanny to two potty-trained boys. Whenever we had to leave the house, they would put up such a fight when I asked them to go to the bathroom. We either wound up being late because we wouldn't get in the car until everyone had at least tried, or I'd just give up and head out the door when, inevitably, someone immediately announced that he *had* to go.

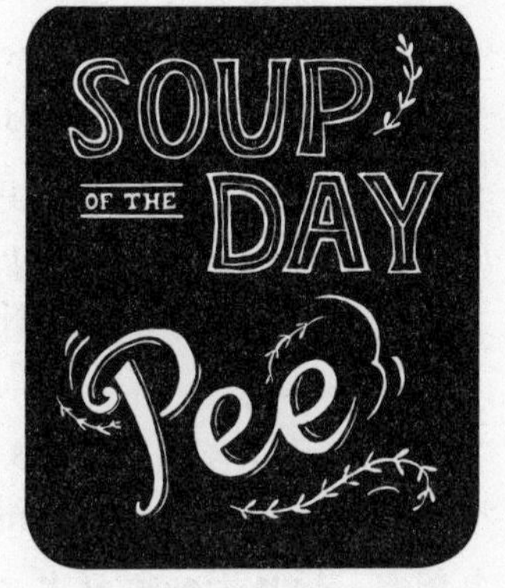

I came up with a trick that came to be known as "Pee Soup." I told the boys to pretend that the toilet bowl was a mixing bowl and we would each add our own "ingredient" as if we were cooking. We would use the bathroom one at a time, myself included, but not flush the toilet, so all of the ingredients could be combined. Sometimes the "soup" was a meal ("I added bacon, his was eggs, now yours can be the hash browns!") and sometimes it was just silly

("This time the soup is mustard, jelly, and Play-Doh!"). The clincher was that after we had all done our business, the boys always wanted to watch as the toilet flushed since that was when the soup got mixed. Was it gross to have three people all take turns peeing into the same toilet without flushing and then looking at what had been created? Yes. Was it less gross than having accidents happen in car seats and on playgrounds? I think so. Did it get the boys to empty their bladders before leaving the house? One hundred percent of the time.

—Meghan, Cherry Hill, NJ

Let me preface this by saying that before I became a mom, I had taken exactly one yoga class in my entire life. When my daughter, now three, was an infant, a local baby yoga class was one of the few things I could figure out to *do* with a six-week-old baby, and so I started regularly attending baby yoga. She enjoyed it so much that as she grew older, we started going to toddler yoga, and now she's a yoga fiend, actually doing poses by name. (No, I still do not attend any adult-only yoga classes.)

The win here is with potty-training. When she poops in the potty, and then stands up, it's hard to actually wipe her clenched butt. However, if you tell her to do Downward Dog, her little butt pops conveniently into the air, and then wiping is a cinch!

—TK, Jersey City, NJ

When potty-training our bright, headstrong, demanding daughter, she wanted to do everything on her own, including wiping! She struggled when wiping her pee—those cute chubby thighs were destined to be in the way. So we incorporated the "plié and wipe" method. Worked wonders and continues to be the most fun thing to say around pottying!

—**KaLeigh, Memphis, TN**

My three-year-old daughter, Nora, was absolutely refusing to sit on the potty even though I was certain that she needed to. After all of my efforts to gain her cooperation fell flat, big sister Lucy came to the rescue. She explained that she was going to be her "service dog" to help her go potty. She dropped to all fours, playfully "barked" and panted, and led an enchanted Nora straight to the toilet seat; she instantly sat and emptied her bladder! —**Erika, Des Moines, IA**

To get my boys to go in the potty, I bought a little gum ball machine and put a jar of pennies in the bathroom. They would get one penny for peeing and two for pooping. They loved the excitement of operating the machine themselves.

—**Lynne, Downingtown, PA**

My three-year-old son has been potty-trained for a while but refused to poop without someone in the bathroom with him. Although it was, at first, adorable to have potty talk with him (our version of pillow talk), I was eager to get him comfortable enough to go independently—so pooping wasn't a forty-five-minute endeavor every evening.

One day, I decided I would try sitting in the hallway and pretend to poop in my imaginary toilet without having a conversation about it. I told him about the imaginary poop I was making, and he was delighted since he loves to pretend. Every time he would try to start chatting about something unrelated,

I just said, "I'm focusing on my poop"—and then I pretend-finished, pretend-wiped, and pretend-flushed and was done. He focused and did the same, except for real. After a few nights of this, he was more focused and more independent about it.

—Joanna, Sudbury, MA

My oldest was scared to go poop in the potty. Finally, we promised that we would take the lid off the toilet tank so he could see what happened when he flushed. He insisted on looking in the tank after pooping for over a year.

—Ann, Grand Rapids, MI

Our two-and-a-half-year-old did great going to pee on the potty while potty-training; however, she preferred number two in her new undies. We'd find her standing quietly in her room pooping in her underpants. One day Daddy helped get her on the potty and said, "Do a poo and we will take a picture and send it to Mommy!" After that she always wanted to poo on the potty and send a picture to the other parent even if we were in the other room. Sometimes she'd run to the living room with my husband's phone to say, "Look, Mom, look at my poop!" She even liked showing her grandparents the picture.

The con: Your camera roll can get really interesting if you don't delete the poo photos right away.

—Sara, Danville, CA

When we were potty-training my youngest daughter, she still loved everything about being a baby. So we turned potty-training into a "baby" activity. We bought her "baby" undies, a "baby" potty, and "baby" treats. When she was successful at using the toilet, we would praise her by calling her a "cute little baby." It totally worked! **—Erin, Boise, ID**

My son desperately wanted to pee into his diaper rather than his training potty. I told him that he might be interested in making "goblin pee"! He was into it. I added one drop of blue food coloring to his potty, telling him that if he peed on it, it would turn green—i.e., "goblin pee." He was thrilled, did it, and was potty-trained! **—Caroline, Falls Church, VA**

My daughter took *ages* to potty-train because she was scared to poop in the toilet. We tried *everything* (rewards chart, bribes, etc.) and nothing worked. She would pee in the toilet and wear underwear all day, but then put on a Pull-Ups diaper when she needed to poop. So I told her we were going to make a tiny hole in the diaper to see if the poop wanted to come out and go into the toilet. We made a small hole with a pencil right where the poop would be, and it was so small no poop came through it the first time. The next time she let me make the hole a bit bigger (as big as an adult thumb), and then a tiny bit of poop peeped out but didn't fall into the toilet. By this stage I had at least convinced her to sit on the toilet while pooping. As the days progressed, the hole got bigger until finally some poop came out and fell into the toilet . . . and she thought it was hilarious! By the end—about five or six days later—the hole was so big the poop just went straight through and our problem was solved! **—Dori, Johannesburg, South Africa**

Table Manners

I buckle my kids into their seats at the dinner table, with belts at the back of the chair that they can't reach. At first, I thought, belts conjure terrible, old-school, hickory-switch-type punishment—or at least have an insane-asylum vibe. It certainly seems like a parenting fail or at least super angry. But they *love* it and pretend to be pilots or astronauts and stay in their seats. **—Rachel, Massachusetts**

My two-year-old is a great eater but not a great sitter. Meals take forever because he's up and down from the table, playing. So I trimmed it up by combining bath and dinner. He has some extra playtime while I prep food and then I feed him his dinner in the bathtub. He's stuck in one spot, occupied, and eats bites when I put them in front of his face. He finishes his whole dinner and gets clean in thirty minutes and it's amazing. And to everyone who is about to shout at me for not teaching him table manners, calm down. My husband works five nights a week, but when he's home for dinner, we do it up right, with cooking and candles and placemats and ritual and togetherness, and my son gets it. But when I'm at it alone, it's my go-to trick for letting him play longer and get to sleep earlier so I can enjoy my dinner and wine over Netflix. **—Elly, Portland, ME**

My partner and I were struggling to keep our kids, three and five years old, engaged at dinnertime. One would be done sitting after ten seconds and would run to play; the other would follow the sibling and dinner would be over.

My partner and I disagreed on what to do. He would expect complacency and demand they sit back at the table even if that meant crying through dinner; I would let them run away because I wanted to enjoy my meal with my partner and not have to deal with the power struggle. The tension between us rose—there was eye rolling and silent judging, and eating as a family was sort of an ordeal.

One day we decided to build a routine into our dinner meals that we could both agree on and let the routine be the boss. We got a twenty-minute hourglass and two candles and placed them at the center of our table. We told the kids that we now have a new dinner ritual, with a few simple rules: Just ourselves and our food at the table (no toys), we sit for as long as the hourglass tells us, and at the end of our meal each kid gets to blow out their candle. Another rule was that no one—not even Mom and Dad—was going to get up. So if you need anything else (milk, salt, etc.), ask for it now. The kids took to this wonderfully and surprisingly quickly. The new ritual did something bigger than get kids to the table—it got us parents in agreement. We even took the hourglass and candles camping. **—Silvia, Portland, OR**

My brother and I had the unsightly habit of talking with our mouths full at the dinner table. We were probably around ages five and eight when my dad decided to combat this behavior with the Elbow Point. Anytime he caught us talking with our mouths full, he would raise his arm and point his elbow in our direction, shouting, "Elbow Point!" The purpose of the Elbow

Point was not to humiliate but to make us aware of what we were doing. It soon became a game where we would all give each other Elbow Points whenever one of us spoke with food in our mouths—we could even catch our parents, which made it fun! When someone had a lot of food in their mouth, we would use both arms for the Double Elbow Point!

—Jaclyn, Ithaca, NY

My toddler kept playing with her milk sippy cup and ended up dropping it on the floor over and over again. I gave her a nice, heavy coaster with those little feet on the bottom so it wouldn't move. Now that there's a "spot" for it, the number of times she's dropped it has decreased by 75 percent because she loves putting it on the coaster like big people. It's been there for six months and still does the trick!

—Meghan, San Luis Obispo, CA

My mom told me it was illegal for children to be too loud in restaurants, and if I started raising my voice, she would say, "Oh, look! I think that's an undercover cop over there!"

—Laura, Wolcott, VT

We decided to learn Spanish together as a family, and my oldest son suggested we do "Spanish Only" dinner one night a week. The first week we tried his idea, none of my kids had any Spanish vocabulary to work with, so nobody fought, complained about the food, or irritated their siblings. They just repeated the few phases I taught them over and over until the meal was done: *"Hola. ¿Cómo está? Estoy bien. Gracias."*

—Tricia, Villa Park, IL

We used to occasionally have No Manners Meals. They were the most fun we ever had at the table until we got older and could joke around more. I suspect it was usually a night when my parents wanted to stop arguing about eating and sitting up straight (and maybe have a beer). We were allowed to blow bubbles in our drinks, put our elbows on the table, eat with our fingers, and best of all, burp out loud. I still vividly remember the sound of Dad always winning the inevitable burping contest, with a reverberating "Burrr-up!"

—**Ginia, San Antonio, TX**

Minimizing Mess

You know all the little crap that kids have around? Stuff from party gift bags and piñatas and Chuck E. Cheese's—it's just everywhere. First I tried throwing it away, but my daughter was obviously upset to see me put the novelty eraser or finger puppet or glitter ball or temporary tattoo in the trash. So then—light bulb! I started collecting all of it into a big glass container with a lid. I see a little piece of crap, I toss it in the jar. Occasionally she asks, "Where is my spinning top with the panda sticker?" and I go get it for her. But usually the jar of stuff just sits and collects. Then it serves three wonderful, useful purposes:

1. If she does something great, she's rewarded with getting to go into the jar and choose something. (Somehow, magically, she never points out that this is all hers anyway.)

2. When friends come over, a special treat is that everyone can choose one thing from the jar. Kids love this! They ask for the jar on repeat visits.

3. For her birthday piñata each year, I fill it with candy, then throw in the entire contents of the jar. It's a little funny to see kids scooping up her spent glow bracelets and partially used sticker sheets, but they are happy and I am happy and other parents have started doing this, too. My daughter has even gotten back one of her old things from another kid's piñata. **—Rebecca, Los Angeles, CA**

One frustrating thing about babies is the game they play of dropping things and watching adults pick them up. The first time Sebastian intentionally dropped something, he was well under a year old, and I just lowered him to the ground and let him pick it up. Over the next few weeks, that evolved to me flipping him upside down and dangling him by his feet to pick up whatever he had dropped—kind of like an arcade crane—so I didn't have to bend over at all. He loved it, and it let him develop his fine motor skills as he worked to pick things up upside down. **—Perry, Boulder, UT**

I recently had a C-section with my second child. As it is difficult to bend, a friend of mine suggested getting a grabbing stick (as in infomercial "I can't reach anything"). I was using it to pick up toys when my three-year-old commandeered it. She has now been using it to clean up all her toys!

—Vicki, Memphis, TN

My seven-month-old daughter is starting to throw her toys and army-crawl everywhere, which makes it challenging to do anything requiring more than one hand and half a brain. So far, she has been completely content when I sit her in a plastic laundry basket with one to three of her toys. She throws the toys, but they stay in the basket, so she can just reach over and get them again. The laundry basket walls are not strong enough for her to be able to pull herself up, so she can't really go anywhere. And I can drag the "baby choo-choo" from one room to another and she just keeps playing.

—TERESA, SOUTHERN PINES, NC

We contain the inevitable mess of toddler play using giant Amazon Prime boxes. Tape the seams and put the toddler in it with a bunch of stickers, markers, crayons, uncooked rice, assorted spoons and containers (for rice pouring); let her trash it as much as she likes until the next order arrives, and she gets a brand-new canvas. —ERICA, BRUNSWICK, ME

I have two sons, ages eight and nine, and they refused to clean their room. I tried everything. I also have a four-year-old girl. She always wants to boss the boys around. One day I told the boys their little sister was their boss until the room was clean. It was clean two hours later. —JINGER, FAIRBURN, GA

This win is a way to get kids to clean up their toys independently, and my mom, Margie, gets full credit—she used it with great success on me and my siblings when we were kids.

It's simple: If the kids clean up the mess 100 percent independently, with no help from any adults, they tell the parent to come look. The parent walks in, looks around, gasps in amazement, and pretends to faint, falling dramatically on the floor.

The parent lies there as if passed out, eyes closed, and only a kiss from the child can magically wake the parent.

—Dorian, Albany, NY

My husband convinced our daughter, who was four at the time, to clean her room so that she could help him bring in and stack firewood. **—Megan, Ithaca, NY**

This is my mom's trick, but I have kept it going with my own kids. After winter break and the gift-giving season, the house is always a mess. New toys or clothes don't have storage places yet, and there is a lot of vacuuming to do and holiday gear to put away. So we used to take New Year's Day to do this, expecting the kids to help. In order to get us to clean up voluntarily, my mom told us a story: The New Year's goat leaves one last present for the kids, but he's shy, so he hides it somewhere in the house. You have to find it in the course of putting things away and tidying up. So when we were almost done putting the house back the way it was before the holidays, my mom would hide one last gift for each of us. It gave us something to look forward to after the letdown of Christmas being over and going back to school, and it was kid-friendly encouragement to help out around the house. Sometimes the gifts were hidden so well, we had to clean things we had never cleaned before just to find them. **—Heidi, Springfield, VA**

Going to Bed and Staying There

On public radio in Canada, we have the 1:00 p.m. time zone signal. It beeps three short dashes followed by a long beep to indicate 1:00 p.m. EST. I told my daughter this was the national nap sound that indicated national nap time, and she and I did not want to disobey the law! We did not want a ticket! Worked like a charm between one to three years of age.

—Anna, Toronto, ON, Canada

My daughter was hazing me: Within a two-hour period, she had touched the side of a building while on a walk and then licked her hand (gross); brushed her teeth with yellow paint (thankfully nontoxic, confirmed with a call to poison control); and then insisted that she "just wanted to sleep all naked" with no diaper. She was two and very much *not* potty-trained. So, with my older daughter watching in utter amusement, I told my younger one that it was too bad she was sleeping "all naked," because I had some really special pj's that I was hoping to give her.

I got a pair of footed pj's that she was pushing growing out of, cut the feet off, put them on her *backwards*—then zipped them up the back, put her in bed, kissed her, and very quietly said to myself, "Go the f*$k to sleep!"

It felt good to both outsmart a very smart and confident two-year-old *and* earn some street cred from my older one.

—Rebeka, Los Angeles, CA

I've gotten my toddler to fall asleep independently by asking him to meet me in a dream. I'll say something like, "Let's go swimming with dolphins in tonight's dream! Meet me there!" He gets super pumped and closes his eyes and I creep out of the room. I still can't believe it works!

—Maggie, Philadelphia, PA

When our daughters were little and would fall asleep in the car, all was well . . . unless the car stopped moving for more than twenty seconds (stop sign = okay; traffic jam = bad). When we'd go on road trips past their bedtimes, we needed them to remain asleep (for all of our sanity), but we also needed to make pit stops from time to time (see again: sanity). And so my husband and I became experts at executing a crazy stunt-driving maneuver.

We'd pause at the rest-stop curb as briefly as possible, and the front-seat passenger would exit stealthily, taking care to barely shut the door (we'd already turned off the interior lights, of course). The driver would then circle the van around the parking lot until the first parent finished his or her business, whereupon we'd "stop" again and, utilizing only the driver's door, the driving parent would exit—essentially *over* the first parent, who was slipping into the seat and bringing the car back up to reasonable parking lot speed ASAP. Once the second parent finished up, there was no official stopping—it was basically just climbing into the passenger seat while the car was still running.

Side note: This was done without speaking, so as to not risk waking the cherubs. **—Emily, Pittsford, NY**

When my daughter was around five or six, my husband started playing a Jim Gaffigan album for her and now she likes to fall asleep to it. She says his voice "soothes" her, and as a bonus, she can recite whole bits of his acts from memory. Last week, we went to the mall and she said, "Look, Mommy, there is Victoria's Secret," and she launched into his act.

—Mary, Camp Hill, PA

When my daughter (age three-ish) suddenly didn't want to go to bed, her teacher recommended I make a chart of sorts: a piece of paper with a line down the middle. On one side, the heading "What Ruby gets to decide," and on the other, "What Mom and Dad get to decide." On the first side, we made a list together: what to wear, what to play with, what plate to eat off of, what music to listen to, and on and on until it was as long as possible. Then on the other side, the short essentials like wearing a seat belt and when to take medicine. But buried in the short list was what time to go to bed.

Every night we would read the chart so that she felt hugely empowered by all the things she gets to do, and we got to tell her in a very sneaky and nonconfrontational way when to get her bum in bed. Then, as things changed, we rewrote the list to emphasize other things we might be having problems with. She's now twenty-one and a delightful human being. And it's all because of the construction paper chart. For sure.

—Gwen, Evanston, IL

Not my win, but my parents' when I was a child: One night, I wanted to play hide-and-seek before bed. My parents told me to go hide under my covers, and they would count to ten and come find me. I loved this game so much that I begged my parents to tell my babysitters to play it with me as well. It wasn't until I was in high school that I realized that they were just trying to get me to go to bed. **—Emily, Chicago, IL**

My five-year-old daughter never wants to go to bed. She wants to stay up and be a part of the action, but my husband and I have that familiar need to "get stuff done" in our last couple hours of the night. Recently I told my daughter what we adults do after she goes to bed . . . dishes and laundry. I told her she is welcome to stay up as long as she wants and do "adult stuff" after hours. She stayed up the first night and folded a basket full of laundry. Now she usually chooses sleep, but when she doesn't, she is up folding laundry or rinsing dishes. Win-win! **—Jen, San Diego, CA**

For years, when babysitting for my niece and nephew, I found I could always get them to bed by creating an ad hoc Bedtime Obstacle Course Game throughout the house (that included a stop in the bathroom for teeth brushing). The "winner" who got to the "finish line" first won a piggyback ride throughout the entire house, which ended in the child's bedroom. It was exhausting for me, but they fell for it every time.

—Janine, Croton-on-Hudson, NY

When we moved from rural Pennsylvania to Brooklyn, our two-year-old son had to get used to a new and much smaller space. His room was directly off the living room, and even after he adapted to living there, he refused to settle down for the night when we tried his old short-and-sweet bedtime routine. My husband, who usually puts him to bed, came up with this ingenious and simple idea: He didn't need a longer routine. Instead, we would all act as if we were going down for the night at his bedtime. It takes less than five minutes. I go into our room and pretend to go to sleep, while my husband walks our son around the apartment, turning off all the lights until he gets to our room, where I get up in the dark to kiss them both good night. The only problem is when we have people over—it's hard to explain to them why they all have to crowd into our bedroom and pretend they're asleep in our bed.

—Julie, Brooklyn, NY

Chapter 4

The Art of Making Monsters Less Scary

On calming active imaginations

WHEN I WAS three years old, I was convinced that a lion lived in my closet. A big ol' hulking lion. Just perched in there with a lion-size red baseball cap and a bright blue T-shirt. There was also a tiger who liked to lie on the shelf beside my bed, right above my record player. These beasts would glare at me menacingly, waiting for me to fall asleep so they could pounce—and, I don't know . . . eat me? I was too young to realize I was already dreaming; they seemed so real.

A lion, a tiger. There must've been a bear, too. At least, according to a sign my mom penned neatly in all caps and taped to my door. It warned:

NO LIONS, TIGERS, BEARS, OR GIANTS ALLOWED IN THIS ROOM!

Giants, I guess, were a bit pouncy, too.

The cool thing is, the sign worked. Those a-hole lions, tigers, bears, and giants stayed away from my room once that piece of paper was posted.

But what about mice, foxes, and wolves?

Ghosts, monsters, robbers?

Those got added to the sign in my mom's same meticulous handwriting—but, with little real estate left on the paper, the new words got squeezed in, smaller than the original admonition. Later, in even tinier letters, she added alligators, crocodiles (just to be sure), witches, and finally, gorillas.

I decorated the sign with stamps featuring covers of children's books and baby animals. Notably, one of the animals was a baby gorilla—maybe that helped to scare off the grown gorillas? Anyway, I think I believed that those stamps would seal the deal. Extra magic to keep the, uh, wolves at bay.

I vividly remember running out of my room in a panic every time another freaky thing started haunting me, demanding that my mom update the list. And without fail, the sign did its job. These were obedient predators. They just needed to be told no.

Apparently, they needed to be told no when I slept in other bedrooms, too. My mom made a quickly scribbled, less pretty sign on yellow lined paper for overnights at Grandma's.

It makes total sense that, as kids, we believe monsters are real. We're told all day by our teachers, our parents, our picture books to trust our imagination. A toilet-paper tube can be a telescope; a cardboard box a spaceship. If you sit in that box with your friend and make-believe hard enough, you can fly to the moon—as simple as Dorothy clicking her ruby slippers and landing back home.

While we're hurtling through space with our preschool pals, our parents are stoking our imaginations with fantasies about Santa and the Tooth Fairy. As a Jewish kid, I learned the truth about Santa early—but the Tooth Fairy? I had seen her. She came to my bed to collect my teeth with a hot dog cart, New York–style. Good thing I hadn't put up a sign to keep her out. Or hot dog vendors.

If benevolent nocturnal visitors are real, why not evil ones? A college friend once told me about her intense childhood fear of the fireplace because, as she told her parents, "If Santa can come down the chimney, so can any old man."

Strangely, the best weapon to fight imaginary creatures is often our own imagination. That's why my No Lions sign worked; I imagined that the words had the power to fend off my enemies. It's absurd, when you think about it—your own imagination battling itself. But comforting, too. Because these battles prove that sometimes when you imagine horrible things into existence, you can just as easily imagine them *out* of existence. Which is an enormous thing for a little mind to do.

Now, sometimes little kids—especially babies—have a hard time differentiating between real and imaginary. And they interpret real things that are actually safe as being monsters.

My daughter screamed bloody murder every time she heard windshield wipers (difficult while driving in a rainstorm) and hand dryers (got funny looks from people waiting to use restaurant bathrooms after us). Sasha's most challenging fear, though, was her fear of family members. For a while, as a baby, she screamed every time she saw my dad or my brother. In general, aside from my husband, Sasha seemed to be afraid of men. She got upset if they'd try to talk to her or hold her—especially if they had facial hair. Matters were made worse when her pal's bearded dad greeted us at the door in a polar bear mask.

I wish I could say I had a win for Sasha's man fear, but the truth is she just outgrew it. I think one day another baby's dad cracked her up with a fake fart, and that was it; they were buds. By the time she was four, one of Sasha's favorite pastimes was to do tricks on her swing set and yell to the male neighbors taking out their garbage or mowing their lawns: "Hey, Barry! Hey, Rick! Look at me! I can do a flip! I can do the monkey bars! Look! Look!"

I do like to think, though, that even if her initial fear was irrational, it's a sign that as she grows, she'll have a healthy skepticism of who deserves her trust.

Fear of Loud Noises

I have a five-year-old and a two-year-old. Both are terrified of noisy public bathrooms (especially those with automatic toilets) and will transition into a full-on tantrum from the moment we enter the stall. I'm talking rolling on the nasty tiled floors and screaming at the top of their lungs. We were in such a situation in the middle-of-nowhere Texas in the summertime, with a long line of women waiting to use the toilets. My kids were screaming, I was panicked because there was nowhere else to pee except among the cactus and fire ants, and everyone was staring at me. I needed to find something to cover the toilet sensor so it wouldn't suddenly flush when one of my kids was sitting on the toilet. In a last act of desperation, I taped a panty liner across the sensor. It worked! Now I never travel without a full bag of panty liners. **—Erica, East Lansing, MI**

We pretend we're fierce animals—lions, tigers, dinosaurs—and roar at the things that are loud or scary.

—Melissa, Austin, TX

I've never liked loud noises—fireworks, balloons popping, thunder. Thunderstorms always woke me up and sent me into my parents' room. They told me the quietest place in the house was on my sister's top bunk (she slept on the bottom) with all the stuffed animals. It wasn't until an earth science class in junior high that I realized it wasn't true.

—LEAH, BROOKLYN, NY

Our two-year-old was starting to become really sensitive to loud noises. That summer, my husband was reconstructing the foundation of our 1860s farmhouse. Read: lots of loud noises at home. So he ordered an extra pair of contractor-grade ear protection and now the little one gets to be just like Dad! He runs to get it when I use the blender, or when my husband is using power tools. Or just any old time he feels like blocking the world out for a bit!

—KAT, PLYMOUTH, VT

I was terrified of thunder and lightning as a kid, and while my parents wouldn't let me come into their bed, they would let me sleep in the windowless bathroom so I couldn't see the lightning. I'd fill the bathtub up with pillows and blankets and sleep there until the storm was over. It was kind of cozy actually.

—TESS, SEATTLE, WA

Fear of the Dark

When I was in high school I taught my much younger brother not to be afraid of the dark. I did this by turning out the lights in my room, making it pitch-black. I then told him to pretend he was a gazelle and I was a lion. He had to hide and I was going to find him—it was scary. Then we switched imaginary animal roles and . . . he wasn't scared anymore. The dark was on his side; he just had to imagine that he was the lion.

—Theresa, New York, NY

I remember when I was a kid, my girlfriends and I used to love to try to scare each other. Whether it was Bloody Mary or Light as a Feather or Ouija. It was fun to try to walk as close as possible to the line of being scared. Being close to scared was kind of like a high for us.

Once, before I had kids, I was with my niece, who was six-ish, at a family dinner. I'd never really been around kids before so wasn't sure what appropriate play was. To understand the context, we were in my aunt's house, which was huge—but all the bedrooms were empty and there were no toys or anything really to play with. So I just thought about what I did when I was a kid, and I made up a game. A game to be *brave*. We would both go in the guest bedroom with the lights off, then close the door. We would hold hands and count to ten. And this would test how brave we could be. When we opened the door, she said, "Let's do it again." I was like, "Okay, now we can do it for fifteen seconds." I just remember how much fun she had playing being brave. **—Julie, Buffalo, NY**

When my daughter was three, she really struggled with sleeping at night because she was scared. After a particularly bad week, out of desperation, I grabbed a spatula from the kitchen and gave it to her. I called it a "magic scepter" that

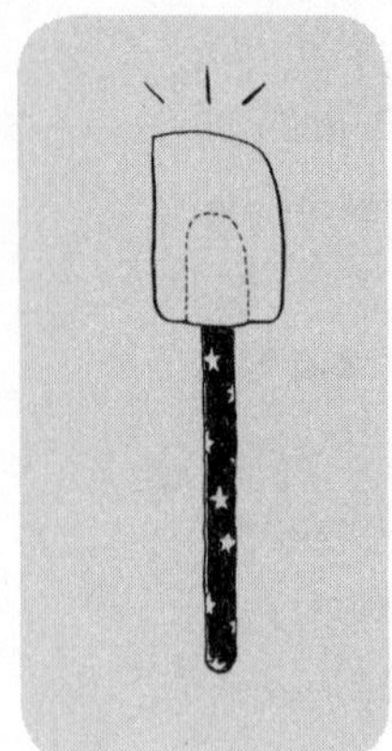

would protect her. Surprisingly, this helped her sleep through the night for several months until she felt she didn't need it anymore!

—Taylor, Richmond, VA

I grew up in an old house, so naturally I was afraid of the dark and ghosts. My dad always told me that the room was exactly the same in the dark as it was in the light. If I was scared, he told me not to hide under the covers but to get up and look at whatever scared me. Go look in the dark closet, go look around the dark corners, and see that you're only afraid of what you think is there.

—Linnea, Maine

When I was a little girl, I was really scared of the dark and of going downstairs to use the washroom in the night on my own. So my dad made up the "Dumb Daddy" song. I would stomp up the stairs singing the "Dumb Daddy" song at the top of my lungs. It was great because it distracted me from being afraid. I would always come back from the bathroom happy, and sometimes I'd even be laughing. Obviously, this would only work for an only child because it was loud and would wake up other kids in the house.

—Alyssa, Toronto, ON, Canada

Fear of Monsters

This is a story that my mother told my two brothers and me as children. When we used to climb into her bed on Saturday morning, we would always see an empty bowl on the floor. Now, we had been told that eating had to be done at a table, of course, not in bed. So we asked my mother why there was an empty bowl next to her bed. She told us this fantastic story about a cute baby dragon who lived under the bed and only came out at night to get food. My mother therefore put out some cereal and yogurt for him in order to fill his appetite. She also wanted to make sure he would not harm us—just in case he was not a vegetarian.

For several years, we made up stories about the dragon under the bed and I still remember them today. A lie that began as a cover for our mother eating in bed had a clear impact on our ability to imagine stories. And we were never scared of dragons. **—Marie, Montreal, QC, Canada**

My six-year-old has a vivid imagination and couldn't get a scary image out of his head. We were in his bed together, and I asked if he would describe the image to me. He started to but got scared all over again. The most I can gather is that it was some sort of monster creature from a cartoon that made a weird noise in a brief cameo. We talked about ways to make the monster not so scary. So, in our minds, we started dressing it up. He suggested a baby bonnet and a pacifier. Then he added a blown-up swimming donut and clown shoes. Soon he was giggling about Minion underwear and lots of bracelets. Next we were talking to the monster, and my son said, "Hey, Monster, how do you like these bananas on your head!?" and shot out his arm like a magician. **—Kelli, Winslow, ME**

My four-year-old son has had difficulty with nightmares since he was about two. Sometimes he'd wake up twice a night, screaming and crying.

My children are also brown—they are mixed race (African, Chinese, Indian, indigenous Guyanese, and, on my side, French Mennonite, of all things). My son loves, loves, loves superheroes, but it's hard to find many brown ones. He does, however, strongly resemble Maui from the movie *Moana*. He is super proud that he and Maui look alike.

After a particularly difficult night with nightmares, I decided to make him a magical Maui hook that mimicked the one Maui uses in the movie. I gave it to him when he came home that night and told him he could use it to battle the monsters in his dream. He sleeps with it near his bed most nights, and we have seen a strong reduction in the number of nightmares he has.

I'm thrilled that this weird tactic worked—*but,* I think it also shows how much brown kids need better brown role models in all forms of media. **—Cate, Salisbury Center, NY**

When I was about six years old, I had terrible nightmares, which led to a real reluctance to sleep. If I had a nightmare, I would run into my parents' room and wake them up for comfort. One time, after a particularly bad nightmare, I woke my dad up, and he told me I just needed to change the channel in my dream.

"How?" I asked, so excited for this revelation.

"You just pull on your ear in your dream, and the nightmare will turn into a nice dream," he told me seriously.

I tried it, and it worked! This also inadvertently led me to learn how to lucid dream, a very handy trick indeed!

—Nico, Redding, CA

When my daughter Kimberly was about five, she suffered from night terrors. One night she came into my bed and was afraid a monster would get her. I laid her on my chest and asked if she could hear my heartbeat. She said she could. I explained to her that Mommy's heartbeats scare the monsters away. She stopped worrying about monsters because she knew my heartbeat would scare them away. She is now twenty-seven with her own wonderful daughter and she plans to tell her the same thing. **—Sonja, Garland, TX**

My three-year-old was struggling to sleep through the night in his own bed, and with a baby on the way, we were on a countdown to get him in his own bed. He claimed that there were scary monsters in his room, which is why he couldn't sleep in there. So we de-monsterfied it by getting giant Sharpies and drawing "protections" on the walls before we painted over it, forever sealing the monster barrier on the wall. We also talked about how the paint was extra stinky and monsters hate that smell. He now sleeps in his own bed! **—Kerby, Naperville, IL**

When my son was afraid of monsters in his room at night, we would send our dog into his room first, before bedtime, and told him that Willow could smell monsters and he would bark and scare them away if there were any. It worked for the fear and made my son love our dog even more.

—Alannah, Maynard, MA

When I was little, I was afraid of witches under my bed. My mom told me that garlic keeps witches away, so I slept with a bulb of garlic on my nightstand. Every few months or so the garlic would "wear out," and I would need a fresh bulb. One night at bedtime, I told my mom that I needed a fresh bulb of garlic, but we didn't have any in the house. But we had some garlic *powder*, and she told me with confidence that powder would work for one night and that we would get fresh garlic the next day. It worked! **—Lydia, Madison, WI**

When my husband was little, he was scared of monsters in his bedroom. My father-in-law made a pretend train ticket and told my husband to give it to the monsters and tell them they needed to board the train and leave. My husband now does this same routine with our three-year-old daughter, Lucy, whenever she gets scared of things like monsters.

—Rachel, Santa Cruz, CA

In the late '80s or early '90s, my family visited the *Queen Mary,* a ship in Long Beach, California. The ship is thought by many to be haunted and the site of paranormal activity. My brother was about five or six and I was nine or ten, and we were all very interested in the haunted aspect. However, when we returned home, my little brother was convinced that ghosts had followed us back from the *Queen Mary.*

He was afraid to sleep alone in his room, so my mom did what any good pre-Internet parent did! She staged a séance in his room to remove any wayward spirits. She lit some candles, grabbed a few pots and pans and wooden spoons, and we all stood in my brother's room chanting to the ghosts to go away and go back to the *Queen Mary*! It did the trick and my brother was satisfied that the spirits had left.

—Haley, San Diego, CA

When I was growing up, I had a genuine fear of monsters under my bed. Knowing that this is pretty typical of kids, my husband and I decided to cut our son's future fear off before it started. Instead of waiting for him to fear what was under his bed, we *put* a monster under his bed. A giant wampa from *Star Wars* to be exact. It looks like a bearskin rug, but in wampa form. It's been there since he was in his crib and is still there at four years old. Now, instead of fearing the monsters under his bed, he knows wampa can handle anything.

—Lindsay, Seattle, WA

Our daughter had been terrified of sleeping in her own bed ever since the "haunted" house led by the fifth graders at our elementary school. She would cry and come into our room repeatedly each night. It lasted for days, until one day my husband suggested that she sleep with a pink souvenir wooden mini baseball bat that he had bought at the Louisville Slugger baseball museum for her a while back. We all laughed about how her family might get bonked in the head if she were to wake up thinking we were a monster, but she readily accepted the idea and now she sleeps soundly, without complaint, in her own bed every night, with her teddy bear and her pink wooden baseball bat next to her. And, so far, no one has been bonked in the head with the pink wooden bat. **—Sarah, Austin, TX**

Monster Deterrents

- Spray made of witch hazel, distilled water, and twenty drops of lavender essential oil (yes, it has to be precisely that many)
- Citrus air freshener (helps with "floating people")
- Peppermint oil (until you accidentally spray it in your kid's eye, and then it stops working)
- Fake spraying sounds
- Daddy's snoring
- Old bike pump (robot blaster for evil robots)
- A few cake sprinkles in the tub
- Bright white teeth (so brush well!)

When my son, Max, was three years old, he started having nightmares every night about Tyrannosaurus rex. He would wake up terrified and screaming, and nothing we said convinced him that T. rex was not an imminent danger. We tried explaining that dinosaurs are extinct. We told him that Mommy and Daddy would not let anything bad happen to him, but he clearly thought we were no match for a ferocious dinosaur. After several weeks of this, we got the idea to try something new.

At restaurants, Max had noticed the No Smoking signs—a picture of a cigarette with a red circle and a line through it—and we explained that they meant no smokers were allowed. That night we went to our computer, found a picture of T. rex, and put a red circle around it with a line across. We taped it to Max's door and told him that meant that T. rex was simply not allowed in his room. Just like he never saw smokers at restaurants with No Smoking signs, he wouldn't ever meet T. rex in a room with a No T. Rex sign. He immediately calmed down, went back to sleep, and never dreamed about T. rex again!

Over the next few years, he would occasionally have nightmares, and we would make a new sign for each new fear (by the time this phase ended when he was around six, there were nineteen signs on his door). His fears ranged from pretty standard (vampires, ghosts) to slightly bizarre (crocodiles with wheels on their feet), but nothing ever lasted more than one night. Once the sign went up, that scary thing no longer bothered him.

—Willow, Chilliwack, BC, Canada

I'm a lot older than my brother. Ten years older. So I basically got to parent him. And also learn from all the mistakes my parents were making. Like this one.

When my brother was two, he loved the tub. So much that he wouldn't get out of it when bath time was over. So my parents invented the Water Monster—which was just that sound of water draining out of the tub when you pulled up the stopper. And it totally worked! Bath time would be over, we'd pull up the stopper, and he'd quickly and dutifully get out of the tub before the Water Monster swallowed him up.

It was playful. But eventually the Water Monster became more monstrous to my brother. We'd pull up the stopper and he would shriek and recoil. We were basically living the shower scene from *Psycho* every night. So my parents invented one more thing—a ritual ceremony that would turn the Water Monster good. At bath time one night, we gathered around the empty tub, my stepdad said a little nonsense incantation, and then he poured a bunch of cough syrup down the drain. That night we lifted up the stopper and my brother had a new friend—the Friendly Water Monster. Someone who gently reminded him, "Hey, buddy, it's time to get out of the bath now. Can't wait to play with you again tomorrow."

—JONATHAN, MONTCLAIR, NJ

Stranger Anxiety

I am not a parent—this is a story about my niece, Billie, and is just about my proudest "parenting" moment since she was born.

I live in Los Angeles, and my sister and her kids live in New York. I see the kids pretty regularly, but a lot of our relationship when we are apart is over FaceTime. Once, when Billie was about three, I arrived for a visit after a long absence. Much to my surprise, this little girl I thought I knew pretty well was immediately scared of me! I tried to hug her, but she ran away and seemed like she was about to cry.

I quickly realized that it had been too long since we'd seen each other for things to be normal right off the bat. She didn't know me as in-person Uncle Jamie anymore—she knew me as FaceTime Uncle Jamie. So I went in the other room and called her. My sister said, "Uncle Jamie wants to talk to you," and Billie jumped right on the phone. We chatted like normal for a second, then I said, "Guess what? I'm here to visit you!" She immediately got excited and started looking for me around the house. It worked! When she found me, all the fear was gone. Suddenly, FaceTime Uncle Jamie and in-person Uncle Jamie were one.

—JAMES, BEVERLY HILLS, CA

Chapter 5

The Art of Keeping Your Kids from Strangling Each Other

On sibling rivalry

HAVE I TOLD YOU yet about my twin sister, Leslie? She looks just like me. But she's meaner. And when she gets mean, her eyes narrow. She says all the things I'm thinking but I'm too nice to say out loud. She has no filter, Leslie.

Other than that, we're exactly the same. Like, *exactly*. Because, well, I *am* Leslie. But my little brother didn't know that.

Josh was six years younger than me, and when he was born it felt like he wasn't just my parents' baby; he was my baby, too. I held him in my lap, fed him bottles, cooed at him, danced with him. Even gave him his middle name. But when my parents weren't looking, I also liked to do things like pull open his eyelids while he was sleeping and watch his eyeballs roll around. I would hold my breath, afraid I might be ruining him forever. Still, I didn't seem to be able to stop myself.

As Josh grew up, I continued to have this split personality thing with him. Doting older sister most of the time; menacing older sister when the spirit moved me. I'd put underwear on his head and snap his picture. I'd stick him inside the cupboard under the bathroom sink, just to see if he could fit (he could). And then, one night, when he lost a tooth, I took it up a notch.

By the time Josh was losing teeth, I was old enough to know that the Tooth Fairy was my mom. Along with the standard under-the-pillow payment, she always used to leave us notes written on a white piece of paper, cut to look like a tooth. She's a calligrapher—even her normal everyday print looks calligraphic—and as the Tooth Fairy, she made zero attempt to conceal her handwriting. One day I was like, "Hey, the Tooth Fairy writes the same as you." She tried to pretend it was just a coincidence. But I knew better.

Anyway, Josh had lost this tooth and somehow there was a lot of blood involved. Which, in my older sister mind, I saw as an opportunity for some fun. That night, I sequestered myself in my room, hard at work at my desk. I got a piece of red construction paper, cut it in the shape of a big drop of blood, and I wrote my own note to Josh. Something about how things go differently when you lose your tooth with lots of blood. There's no Tooth Fairy. There's the Bloody Fairy. She takes your tooth and leaves you nothing. Nothing but this note.

I stayed up, waiting until my mom had done her Tooth Fairy thing. When I was sure my parents were asleep, I snuck into Josh's room, took my mom's note and the money from under the pillow, and stealthily replaced them with the Bloody Fairy's message.

The next morning, I awoke to anguish from Josh and disappointment from my parents. I was forced to come clean to him and apologize. Though I was not to come clean about the Tooth Fairy, who they assured him would visit that night.

I did not like being chastised by my parents. And I knew I'd done something bad. But it felt good to be bad. And I realized if I wanted to get away with it, I just had to be sneakier.

Thus, Leslie was born.

She'd show up randomly next to Josh's car seat on the way to the town pool. In the backyard, playing in piles of leaves. At night, wrestling on my bed. She was her worst when our parents would go out, leaving me (ahem, Leslie) in charge. I don't remember exactly what Leslie would tell Josh, and neither does he. I just know that my voice would get a little whispery and I'd say something like, "If you keep playing with that light switch, Mom and Dad will never come home."

"You're Leslie," he'd say tearfully. "I can tell because your eyes are squinty."

In retrospect, yes, I feel a little remorse over Leslie. But I also think having a sibling is a chance for people to experiment with what happens when we're mean to another person. How to reconcile and make it up to them. Leslie only ever showed up in tiny spurts—and when I came back as Hillary, I couldn't wait to take Josh for wagon rides, teach him hard-to-pronounce words, and bore my friends to death with stories about how cute he was.

My mom says she lucked out in the fact that Josh and I didn't really have any sibling rivalry (haha, sorry, Mom). And she thinks the reason we got along so well was because she had us so far apart; she basically had two only children.

I myself have an actual only child. I like it that way. But it means my daughter doesn't get the benefit of being a Leslie or having anyone Leslie her. We have to look outside our home to find opportunities for the intense bonding and friction that many children get from their siblings. I've been lucky enough to live in a town with plenty of only children. The cool thing about knowing other parents with onlies is, there is an implicit understanding that we can use each other's kids as babysitters. Drop-offs are great. But for me, even having another child over at my house is a big parenting break. Occasionally, I'll get a text from another mom saying, "Hey, can I borrow Sasha for a couple of hours? I've gotta get some cleaning done." And I totally get it.

The funny thing is, I feel a twinge of deep satisfaction when I hear these only children bickering on playdates. I don't even mind when they shout at each other—though I barely have any tolerance for Sasha shouting when she's friend-free. I mostly tell the kids what I've heard parents tell kids when they're fighting with their brothers and sisters: Find a way to work it out. Usually, they do. Sometimes, they just can't, and the win is that the children can retreat to their own homes and start fresh on the next playdate. One mother told Sasha recently, "My daughter is like a snail. She needs to go back in her house sometimes. But she'll be ready to play again soon." Which I thought was a lovely way to normalize the heartbreaking experience of your friend getting sick of you—which most siblings experience frequently but is maybe less expected from a nonrelative.

Since I've never had a sibling close in age and my daughter will never have one at all, I'm going to leave the actual sibling rivalry wins to the wonderful people who submitted anecdotes in this chapter.

And lest you think the moral of my Leslie story is that older siblings always win, I offer you this: On my tenth birthday, we went mini golfing, and on an overly enthusiastic backswing, my little brother clubbed me in the face, knocking out a chunk of my tooth and leaving me with a gigantic swollen lip.

Just days before I started middle school.

This New Baby Is BS

My husband and I had our second son six years after our first was born. With so much time between them, my oldest son has had a lot of one-on-one time and years of being my favorite human.

When his brother was born, my oldest starting having behavior issues. I expected the regression and tried my best to be patient and loving through the fits. At the same time, though, my oldest started talking about himself negatively. He would tell me that he was stupid (which he isn't), that he was mean (also not true), and that nobody liked him (breaks a mama's heart).

I tried everything I could think of to get through to him that he was still loved and important. We read books about older siblings, went on dates without little brother, celebrated him as an individual, and explained that the baby did not change how I felt about him. None of it worked.

Finally, one day, while we were driving home from church and listening to him tell me that he was dumb, something in me snapped. I couldn't stand anyone talking about my Sweetness that way—even him—so I broke a parenting rule I had set for myself: I told my oldest that he was my favorite. He got quiet for a couple of minutes and then said, "I'm not really your favorite, Brother is." I responded, "No, he isn't. I get to pick who my favorite is, and it is you."

Since that day, my oldest has stopped throwing fits. He has stopped the negative talk, and he has started listening to us again. I truly believe that my guy just needed to know he was still loved. That his brother was not a replacement for him, and that he was still my favorite human—even if that isn't exactly true.

The truth is, my favorite can change by the minute. For the most part, I don't have a favorite. But there are the car rides when the baby screams for half an hour straight while my oldest tries to soothe him with songs, or the dinners when my oldest refuses to eat while his brother gives me toothless grins—and for just a moment I truly do have a favorite.

I hope the baby never feels that I love his brother more than him, but if that day comes, I will simply tell him the same thing I told his brother: "I get to pick my favorite and it is you." And I will continue to pray that I am not breaking my children's psyche. **—Danielle, Bremerton, WA**

My older child, two and a half years old, was suffering from conflicted feelings when my second child was born. At the hospital, he snuggled with the baby and seemed happy to be a big brother. But when we brought the baby home, he refused to come into the house to see the baby. He referred to the baby as "no-no."

So I went upstairs, put the baby in his carrier seat, placed the seat in a hallway closet, went outside, and told my oldest that I had lost the baby. "Can you help me find him?"

Older brother bounded up the stairs, searched two bedrooms, and then heard a cooing sound coming from the closet. He opened the door, saw his brother, and beamed. "I found the baby!" he exclaimed.

Older brother knelt down and gently patted the baby's head. Within a few minutes, he fell in love with his younger brother and became protective of him. Older brother has been devoted to his little brother ever since.

—Mary Beth, Washington, DC

We have a new baby in the house, which means our nine-year-old son has been acting out in really ridiculous ways—throwing himself on the ground and then screaming that he's hurt, singing annoying songs at full volume. He isn't self-aware enough to identify that he's feeling left out and insecure, or to just ask us directly for attention. So we've started to ask if he would like some attention from us, and then the whole family gives him a round of applause. We go from ignoring him because we're focused on baby to giving him fifteen seconds of full attention and praise. This has been a great stopgap for getting him "unstuck" when he's feeling neglected.

—Biff and Trystan, Portland, OR

The best tip someone gave me about bringing our second home was to speak to the newborn baby the same way we would speak to our oldest about having to wait and be patient until we were finished with something. So the baby would literally be sitting in the Rock 'n Play sleeping, and I'd say, "Baby Max, you're going to have to wait a few minutes while I finish reading this book to Charlie." Or "Baby Max, I will be with you in a second, but right now I'm playing trucks with Charlie." It helped my older kiddo because he got to see that he wasn't the only one who had to wait his turn and be patient; the baby had to wait as well. It felt a little ridiculous at the time since the baby was just sitting there, not needing or wanting anything, but it honestly really helped. I could see the look on my oldest's face when I would say those things to the baby. He felt like his time was being honored even though so much had changed since the baby had arrived. **—Mary, La Grange, IL**

Our son was almost four when our daughter was born. I solicited tons of advice for how to keep our connection strong during this transition. I got a mini trampoline so he could go crazy when I was stuck inside nursing. I got lots of books for him, because I was delusional and thought I could read out loud and nurse at the same time.

I suggested that the new baby wouldn't be able to do any of the cool things he could do (run, jump, paint, climb, use a fork) and that maybe he might like to teach her some things. He thought about it and decided the most important thing he could teach her would be to march. To my knowledge he had maybe marched once or twice in his life, but he latched on to this idea and even marched around her once or twice to "show her how it's done." No instruments, no music, just one determined little boy, marching around a newborn.

Two years later, we sometimes use this strong desire to show what he knows when we really need them to cooperate. She adores him and (to his dismay) wants to do everything he does. **—Ginia, San Antonio, TX**

My son is five, my daughter one and a half—so while he is very into playing out elaborate scenarios with *Star Wars* figures, she is into snatching them from their positions and brutalizing them in some way. To prevent him from losing his mind and lashing out at her every time she interrupts the game, we have taken to shouting: "Oh, no, the rancor is attacking!" This has yielded remarkably good results in terms of them being able to play together; however, our son now also introduces his sister to strangers as "the fearsome rancor."

—Luise, Brisbane, Australia

I Win!

This win is called “the DJ.” It all started when my kids were about two and four. The kids would fight over what music we’d listen to in the car. I decided to deem one of them the DJ for the day, which meant he or she could pick the music. This morphed into having a daily DJ, with first dibs on everything. My seven-year-old son is the DJ on Tuesdays, Thursdays, and Saturdays. My five-year-old daughter is the DJ on Mondays, Wednesdays, and Fridays. The DJ gets to have their favorite plate at breakfast, the first choice of blanket or pillow for TV or snuggle time in the living room, and the pre-dinner video, bedtime book, etc.

Some notes: My hubby and I are the joint DJ on Sundays . . . woo-hoo! And if a kid is misbehaving or making a big deal about getting to pick first, he or she can lose DJ privileges for the day. Occasionally, a kid can earn a bonus DJ day on Sunday for especially good or kind behavior.

—Maureen, Presque Isle, ME

The sad reality became obvious to our second son when he was three or four that he was going to come in second in just about everything compared to his big brother—running races, competitions to do anything fastest. The magic solution? His older brother, who was only five or six years old, invented the title of “first second.” As in, he would be first, but his little brother could achieve “first second.” After all, he was the first one to come in second each time!

—Joanna, Westford, MA

My kids were always turning everything into a race: who could get down the stairs first, who could get to the car first, who could reach the front door first. It resulted in endless tears. The younger one couldn't keep up, the one who declared the race was already halfway to the destination, one would shove the other out of the way.

So I invented Second One Gets the Hug.

It's simple: If they race, whichever kid comes in second (the loser, since we have two kids in our family) gets a hug from Mom and a reminder, "Second one gets the hug."

Whoever came in first started to get really jealous.

It didn't take long until they were saying to each other, "After you!" "No, you go first!" because they both wanted hugs. I had to add a rule that if they were *exceedingly* kind and patient with each other, they could both get hugs.

—**Dorian, Albany, NY**

Every kid loves a new toy, but as parents we're always encouraging them to share. Well, the day my kids got something new, they had the power to share or not to share.

The scene: My son finally puts down that new Transformer to go to the bathroom. He comes back to find his little brother twisting the toy into a new shape. You know what happens next. Tears. Maybe a shove or a wrestling match.

Instead, my kids would just say, "First day!" and the toy had to be handed over. No sharing required. Because everyone loved their first-day security, each learned to honor it with their siblings.

—**Sonja, Hardwick, MA**

I have twins. Around the time they turned three, the conflict between them reached a new high. They jockeyed for the favored position for those all-important child privileges like: who gets to push the elevator button, whose story gets read first at bedtime, who gets to pick the movie for family movie night, and who gets to cuddle in the middle of Mommy and Daddy's bed in the morning (and who gets relegated to Mommy's right side on the edge of the bed). The morning my daughter body-checked her brother into the dresser in order to beat him to the prized spot, I knew we had to come up with something. Here's my win, born out of the bumps and bruises of sibling conflict: If you have two kids, assign one even, the other odd. Then whenever there's a question of who gets the "advantage," it's decided by what day it is. Who gets their pick of car seat? Odd kid, because today's the third. Who gets the last hug at drop-off? Even kid, because today's the sixteenth.

—Suzanne, Oak Park, IL

When it's snack time, I will give one of the kids two crackers (or fruit snacks or what have you) and instruct him to keep one and give his brother the other. They have to practice sharing, but also learn to trust each other. It feels good when your brother gives you something (because how often does that happen?) and to hear a thank-you from your brother (because how often does that happen either?). It's a small thing, but it has been amazingly effective. **—Jackie, Helena, MT**

My younger brother and I fought often when we were young, especially between the ages of six and ten. We even used to fight over who got to massage our mom's feet! My mom had somehow convinced us that we could help her out by massaging her feet and that it would also be really fun. Luckily my mom has two feet so my brother and I were each able to massage a foot. Everyone won . . . sort of . . . mainly just my mom.

—Stephanie, Seattle, WA

Very Important Things Siblings Have Argued About

- Who gets to have "the point" from the top of a new container of margarine
- Do dinosaurs go to heaven or hell?
- Whether there is a right and left sock
- Who gets to hold the Costco receipt
- Whether Mom will let them drive the car (ages eight and three)
- Who gets to wear the good jeans
- Who gets the spoon with the stars on the handle
- Who farted (they both claimed it)

Bickering

Driving in the car, my two daughters were fighting horribly and making me crazy. I finally yelled, "Quiet! All of you. We're entering the Tyrannosaur paddock." Sort of like Muldoon's line in *Jurassic Park*. I told them we were navigating a dinosaur park with dinos on the loose. They behaved the rest of the drive, imagining they were seeing the different dinosaurs and pointing them out to each other as we drove. Occasionally, I pretended I saw one in my rearview mirror and we were outrunning it.

—Kaleena, Bothell, WA

I have three kiddos—eight, eleven, and fourteen. And while they often get along with each other quite well, we definitely have our share of angry car rides home from school, grumpy sibs at dinner prep time, and the like. Several years ago, I discovered that when one or more of them needs attention, redirecting, or argument solving that I can't instantly give, I could put on Christmas music. Any time of year! I don't ask if anyone wants Christmas music or say anything; I just walk to the nearest device, turn on "Rudolph," and the magic is almost instantaneous. My eight-year-old and I are listening to a mixed Christmas album right now, which totally stopped her impending tantrum. She's singing along to "White Christmas" and I am breathing a sigh of relief!

—Megan, San Diego, CA

My parents used to play the Life Savers game on long car trips: Each child gets a Life Savers candy, and whoever can make it last the longest wins a second Life Savers. I didn't realize until I was much older how quiet a child is when they spend all their effort trying to keep the Life Savers from dissolving. I think it gave my parents a nice break from bickering on long car trips. **—Elizabeth, Portland, OR**

We usually get our groceries delivered, so we often have cardboard boxes lying around. When my kids are getting in each other's way, especially around mealtime, I give them each a box to decorate and turn into a spaceship. Then we have Spaceship Dinner, where they each eat in their own self-contained private space. **—Miriam, Philadelphia, PA**

When my kids are fighting incessantly, I ground them . . . from playing with each other. I tell them they have to play quietly *alone* for fifteen minutes or so. Soon, they are whispering around the door to each other and passing notes, and I semi-sternly remind them of the grounding. Then, after the time has elapsed, I let them off their "grounding" and they play happily. Weirdos. **—Elizabeth, Overland Park, KS**

I have four kids—one biological son and three stepsons. A few weeks ago, my husband was away on a business trip. I had been solo-parenting for a week, and it was the first week back to school! The kids were at one another's throats, and I was sooooo tired of breaking up fights. After some deep breathing and a personal time-out for myself, I got a sudden burst of inspiration. I gathered the kids in the living room and announced that today just happened to be all of our Unbirthdays and that we were going to have a party to celebrate. They all loved the idea and we spent the next several hours decorating the house, baking a cake, and making handmade gifts for each other. The kids worked together to make an Unbirthday sign with all of our names on it, came to an agreement on the type of frosting for the cake, and showed real kindness to one another when we played party games. I made each of them—and myself—a card that showed how many days old we each were and wrote in it something I appreciated about them. We all had a marvelous time and agreed that we needed to do

it every year. That day I felt that I really was the mom I wanted to be. **—Suki, Bellingham, WA**

I have two kids, four and six, who share a room. Lulu is a night owl and Holden wants to sleep right away. They have bunk beds. We let Lulu take a small flashlight and stack of Magna-Tiles to bed with her so she can play quietly and leave her brother alone. The flashlight has a solar charge so we don't have to worry about her leaving it on all night and using lots of batteries. **—Heather, Phoenix, AZ**

I have four children. Two are the same age, born in 1980, and two are a year apart—born in 1983 and 1984. When the kids were together, invariably something would break or something would cause all four of them to start yelling at one another. I would ask them, "Who did it?" but I'd always get four fingers pointing in four directions.

This would upset me because they had all gotten away with lying *and* covering for each other at the same time. One day, instead of asking who did it, I asked them in my loudest Mommy-is-mad voice, "Who DIDN'T do this?!!" The kids were stunned. They looked at each other very curiously and one after the other came right out with the guilty kid's name.

That trick never failed, but I only had to use it a few times. Eventually the kids began confessing themselves. Because they learned it was okay if something got broken or misplaced.

—Denise, Huntington Beach, CA

In our blended family, our daughters are barely a month apart in age. They have radically different interests and we enjoy finding common ground, even for one afternoon. Combining their love for the outdoors with my imperative that they learn a second language, I decided on a Spanish-language hike. At every turn of the uphill trail, we stop and rest. I bring a pack of M&M's. To get any, they need to ask me for the correct color using Spanish. *Rojo! Amarillo!* In this way, they learned colors. *Por favor. Gracias. Por favor, dame un dulce rojo. Vamos. Ahorita. Arriba!* **—Karen, Albion, CA**

My daughters, eighteen months apart, hit the age where they were embarrassed by me at almost the exact same time that they started bickering endlessly.

Anytime they start to argue in public, I threaten to start singing if they don't stop. Works 100 percent of the time.

—Amy, Northampton, MA

When my brother and I were old enough to stay at home alone, our parents paid both of us to babysit ourselves. The deal was, if we fought or there was trouble, no one would get a cent. We did great together and never had an issue when it was just the two of us. Obviously, we both wanted the cash, but I'd like to think the responsibility of "you need to take care of you" encouraged us to rise to the occasion. **—Sher, Minnesota**

I became a stepmother of two beautiful girls when I married my husband. I was excited and nervous, much like a new mom, but with the added stress of sharing kids and navigating co-parenting. I didn't have the biological advantage of parental authority that comes with the aches and pains of pregnancy and labor and delivery, but what I did have was the creative experience of growing up in a family of six. I remember when my siblings and I would fight or fuss, my parents would find ways of forcing us to spend more time with the sibling we weren't getting along with—like sitting in the same room in silence looking at each other.

This summer, when our girls were fussing and fighting, my creative juices started flowing. After a particularly long morning at the pool, where they were not getting along and being unkind to each other, we arrived home and I issued a Sibling Challenge. The Sibling Challenge was a task they had to do together. They had to use kind and encouraging words and take their time and do their best work for the challenge to be completed. The challenge was putting the groceries away in the fridge. They had to sort the groceries into categories, make sure there was enough space for everything, and clean up after themselves. After I gave the instructions, I told them if they didn't complete this Sibling Challenge with encouraging words and cooperation, there would be another one until they could learn to work together. They completed the task well and with kindness, and for the rest of the day there wasn't any fussing or fighting.

As a stepparent, I find discipline the hardest hurdle to overcome. It is easy to become overwhelmed with fear and worry about whether you are doing the right thing and whether they will go to their other house and say how horrible it was to be at your house; but regardless of how long you have your children, you have to do your best to teach them to be kind and caring human beings. Sibling Challenges are just a little way for us to remind our girls that they have to depend on each other as they travel back and forth from house to house.

—Merianna, Columbia, SC

Chapter 6

The Art of Keeping Your Cool

Like, whenever possible

OKAY, SO THIS ONE isn't my strong suit. I'm the kind of person who holds it all in, holds it all in, holds it all in . . . until I just can't anymore, and I blow.

On a good day, I catch myself before it happens and I run into the kitchen and scream into a dishtowel. Or hide in the pantry and stuff my face with my daughter's animal crackers and wash them down with a box of her chocolate milk. Ahh, much better!

Over the years, I've learned that things work best if I let out a little steam at a time rather than waiting till I burst. But old habits don't die easily. And the holding-it-in moments can be so incremental that I don't notice a top-blowing moment sneaking up on me.

One night, after my daughter was in bed, I stumbled upon something that diffused some of that holding-it-in-ness. My husband was at work late and I was flipping around on the TV, looking for a rom-com—preferably with Jennifer Aniston. Something I knew he'd never agree to watch with me. I didn't find the chick flick of my dreams, but I saw that Jill Soloway's *Afternoon Delight* was on. A mom friend had told me I had to see it, so I decided tonight would be the night.

I won't spoil it for you—you really should see it—but it's about these two parents trying to navigate their relationship and their identities and their friendships and the judgment of other parents and their sex life and the looming question of will they or won't they have another child. It was all feeling very familiar. So familiar that I broke down bawling. Like, the kind that makes you glad you're seeing this movie at home and not in a theater.

After that? I felt great. I mean, yeah, I was like, *Man, I guess I've got some shit to work through.* But the tension that had been ravaging my body got knocked down a few notches. And the next day I had more patience for my daughter.

Since then, I've gotten better at recognizing when I need a Big Cry. Maybe it would help for me to hire an acting coach who could teach me how to cry on command. But since I'm more wired for stoicism than emotional outbursts, when I feel the stress building, I'll sit down on the couch and channel surf for tearjerkers. Usually it works best if the show or movie is about parenthood. But in a pinch, a sappy rom-com will also do the trick. Thanks, Jennifer Aniston!

Also, when you drop your child off at activities, if you have the opportunity to wait in your car, I highly recommend setting an alarm to go off five minutes before the class ends and sleeping as long as you can! It's amazing how far a little nap will go in buying you some patience.

Blissful Distraction

We saw so many parents losing their cool with kids on airplanes—kids needing to move, really, and parents stressed. So when we had our little one, we started bringing non-inflated balloons with us to the airport. Takes up no room in our carry-on. We inflate a balloon when waiting to get on the plane, then little one runs, batting it around, hitting it at windows, and getting those wiggles out. When done, just pop it (quietly) and throw it away before getting on the plane!

—Beth, La Crosse, WI

My three-year-old is really trying out being Mr. Mean lately and not Mr. Cooperative. I realize that sometimes he gets stuck in the less-than-ideal behavior and has trouble coming back, even though he wants to. It's hard not to lose my patience. But I recently thought of that jokey thing you do when you move your hand down in front of your face and then reveal a different face when your hand comes away. I did this for my son and then asked if he wanted to try, too. He went from an angry frown to a genuine smile and it completely brought him (and me) back from the brink. Now it's our new go-to!

—Ami, Brooklyn, NY

Afternoons at home with four kids (ages one to eight) can get long. Four irritable kids and one crabby mom is a recipe for sibling rivalry and power struggles. This often results in my alter ego, Demon Mommy, making an appearance. Attempting to keep her at bay, I invented the Child-Abuse Prevention Drive (CAP Drive for short). It goes like this: Everyone is buckled in to their strategically placed car seats/boosters in the minivan. We put on some good music or a favorite podcast and head to the nearest drive-through. We get fueled up on grease and sugar and head out. Sometimes we just drive around the neighborhood, but I have driven as much as an hour out of town if the kids are asleep. It keeps everyone separate so no one gets hurt, it kills time, and it definitely calms me down as I sit alone and untouched in the front seat, enjoying my coffee and a drive-through treat. **—Elizabeth, Sacramento, CA**

When my eldest was going through a super-whiny toddler stage (and I was sleep-deprived from a new baby), I decided to start putting bow ties on my toddler. It's virtually impossible to lose it on a toddler in a rainbow bow tie!

—Natalie, Peterborough, ON, Canada

I use a mobility scooter to get around. It is a challenge to keep track of, keep in line, and keep up with my young school-age daughter while shopping. It seems like I'm constantly reprimanding her or almost running over her toes! So I let her sit on my lap instead, which is a big hit—for both her and all the ogling shoppers that we pass. She understands firsthand that it's *not* a toy, and being involved helps normalize my mobility aide—a win that hopefully translates into a larger lesson as she grows! **—Rachel, Middleton, WI**

When my baby is frustrating me, I call her "baby" instead of her name to remind myself that she's a baby and is not trying to push (figurative) buttons. It calms me, centers my focus on being her parent, and tends to remind me that I desperately want her in my life (we had a lot of miscarriages before she arrived). —Catherine, Strasbourg, France

My husband and I always dreaded the "bewitching hours" with our super-colicky baby. No matter what we would do, he would scream from 5:00 to 7:00 p.m. Since he would cry no matter what we did, we would put him in the stroller and make a stiff drink. It was easier to handle the screaming outdoors. We would sip our cocktails while hoping our neighbors wouldn't call Child Protective Services. We called this our nightly "cockwalk" (or "walktail" if we were trying to be more appropriate). —Chelsea, Grass Valley, CA

Role-Playing

When I feel like I'm about to lose my shit with my three-and-a-half-year-old daughter, going into "character" mode is often a surefire way to defuse the situation, insert humor, and get her to do what I want her to do. This morning when she was underneath the kitchen table and I needed her to put her shoes and coat on, pee, and get out the door, I asked her which characters we should be and she assigned me the mean witch and herself Glinda. It makes it fun for her, but more important, it reminds me to laugh and gives me a healthy distance from the whole situation. —Sarah, Northampton, MA

I am a special-ed teacher and was working in a population of students, ages eight to fourteen, with severe autism. Transitions were always hard for us, especially when they were not standard routines. My class was on one of our first monthly field trips to the pool at the YMCA. My students loved swimming but often needed coaxing to get in and out of the pool. We supported these transitions with social stories (books designed specifically to help understand certain events), visuals, and warnings about upcoming shifts—but they're often still tricky.

One of my students was a self-proclaimed animal expert. He was charming, hysterical, and had indeed taught us all a significant amount about animals, ranging from the common to the exotic. On this particular day, the rest of our class had already gotten out of the pool and were making their way to the dressing rooms, then to the bus, all while he was still splashing around in the water. I was getting desperate, and given that he was a strong thirteen-year-old boy, I wasn't about to carry him out. I had to get creative. I asked what he knew about sea turtles—how they move in water. He gave a beautiful reenactment. Then I asked what he knew about how they lay eggs. If you know anything about sea turtles—which I now did, thanks to my fabulous animal expert—you know they go on land to lay their eggs. He started to describe this to me. I asked him to *show* me, but he wasn't taking the bait. So instead I took a risk and tried to follow his verbal directions, acting out a sea turtle laying eggs . . . on a pool deck . . . at the YMCA . . . in front of lots of strangers. I intentionally made errors as I went. Finally, laughing at his ridiculous teacher who couldn't follow his simple directives, he got out to show me how. We laid eggs the entire way to the changing room.

During our next trip to the pool, each student was asked to choose an animal mascot for the trip and was called to show off their skill at the end. My "sea turtle" and I had no problems getting out on time after that! **—Kristina, New York, NY**

When I'm about to lose it with my three-year-old daughter, I will start talking to her in a really bad French accent. "Oh, Mademoiselle Shelby, you must feel so rebellious to pee in your hand in the toilet. *Ma chérie,* we must wash the urine from your hand . . ." and so on. Taking on another persona helps me keep my cool, and it's kind of fun! **—Jenny, Stanfield, NC**

Like most parenting wins, this started with a parenting failure. As my son neared his first birthday, nursing was not slowing down. He started demanding "boo!" Or even a nice, clear "boob!" in public. I wish I had taught him "nurse" or something else. But "boob" it is. Now, as a toddler, he wants boob all the time and I cannot handle the whiny begging every half an hour. One day, I answered him in a terrible Freud impression, "Ah, yes, boob. Vat is the problem? Tell me all about the boob. Did your mother deny you the boob as a child? I believe this to be the root of your unhappiness." And so on. It doesn't stop the whining, but it keeps the situation from escalating by keeping my cool. I do this with the six-month-old I have for daycare now as well: "Ah, yes. It is clear to me zat your problem is tired. There is a proven cure for dis, though. It is simple. It is sleep. Zat is all you must do!" **—Colleen, Anchorage, AK**

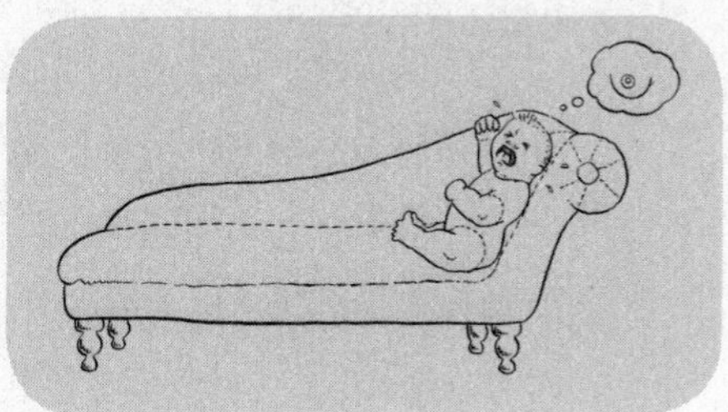

I had my younger son convinced he had a battery pack, and when he got too wild while playing, I would call him over and remove his batteries (I would open the door on his back, remove them, and then close the door back up) and he would cool down for a while. He never asked for them back, but he was always ready to have them removed. It only worked until he was about five, but it was great while it lasted. He is nineteen now and still remembers his batteries being taken out. **—Tracy, Nashville, TN**

Parenting Mantras

"Screaming is breathing."

—from a mom whose first child was stillborn, to get her through challenging moments with her screaming children

"But not today"; for example, "The laundry has to get done . . . but not today." —from a mom whose husband was deployed

"This is the last [day of the week] when my baby is [age] and [whatever the hard thing is]"; for example, "This is the last Thursday when my baby is six months, three weeks old and won't nap because he's overtired."

"This isn't crazy; this is just my crazy."

—from a dad, reminding himself that everyone deals with their own flavor of crazy

"My life will not always look this way."

Giving In to the Rage

My kids are six and three and, like most, don't like to go to bed. The nightly ritual of getting them upstairs can be hellish. One night, my husband was out at a meeting and I'd already had a rough afternoon of the kids not listening. I told them for the eighty-seventh time it was bath time and they ran behind a couch to hide and laugh hysterically. I felt like yelling and throwing things. So, I did. I yelled (legitimately yelled), "Raaaaawwwwww. Bath monster smells stinky boys! I eat stinky boys!" I chucked the pillows they held over their heads and stomped around them. Slightly terrified and slightly exhilarated at Mom's new voice, they ran upstairs with me chasing them and jumped in their bath, nervously giggling. This is one of those techniques you can only pull out in dire situations, maybe quarterly. It really felt good to scream though.

—Kelli, Winslow, ME

I allow myself to cry until snot bubbles come out and I pick up the pieces after that. Ice cream also helps!

—Sandra, Vancouver, BC, Canada

One Sunday I was super tired of my children—two boys, ages five and two—and I happened to be wearing a hooded sweatshirt. The kids had been in my face all day and I wanted to hide, so I put the hood over my head and said, "Go away. Mommy's on vacation." To my amazement, my older son looked at his brother and said, "Brendan, Mom's on vacation. Let's play upstairs." It was magical. A little while later, he peeked downstairs and I quickly put my hood back up. "Oh, no, not yet," he called back to his brother. "She is still on vacation!" And now, miraculously, every time I make this announcement, as long as I have a hood to pull up, I am allowed a mini vacation from parenting. **—Elizabeth, Metuchen, NJ**

I made up a song about my alter ego called "Nutso Mommy, Not So Nice Mommy" to defuse difficult parenting situations and to help us all have a little laugh. The first time I went on and on and had a whole song and dance. Since then, I just have to sing "Nutso Mommy, Not So Nice Mommy" and they giggle and we move on. **—Megan, Burlington, VT**

When it's just too much, the house is too crowded, and the mood is getting too cranky, we stop and do a Family Scream. Sometimes we've already been yelling, sometimes we are in the car, sometimes out in public. We stand facing each other and, on the count of three, just throw our heads back and send a bloodcurdling scream into the sky. It would make sense to hold hands, but we are usually clenching our fists! It's quick, cathartic . . . and it works. **—Kate, Shorewood, WI**

My kids are ten, six, and three. Occasionally when I catch myself yelling, I turn it into an outrageous threat so we all start giggling, like "IF YOU KEEP DOING THAT I'M GONNA . . . HANG YOU FROM THE CEILING FAN BY YOUR TOENAILS!" **—Angela, Denville, NJ**

Not Giving In to the Rage

One hot summer day, my kids, about six and eight at the time, were repeatedly put in time-out for bickering. I was ready to lose my cool, when I had a moment of clarity: *I needed a time-out from my kids!* So, when the next conflict arose, I said, "Holy cow! I am so frustrated; I'd better go to time-out before I get *so* angry I say something I shouldn't! SO MOMMY IS IN TIME-OUT! I must stay in my room for ten minutes, with the door closed. I may *not* talk to anyone until I calm down and I can*not* come out until I am ready! DO NOT LET ME OUT!"

My kids were so hopelessly, beautifully speechless as I went to my room. I stayed in there for ten minutes with the door closed—not even the dog was allowed to come in to see me. It was silent outside my door and the kids lost interest in whatever they were nitpicking about. When I came out, I told my kids I felt much better and I hoped we were all ready to move forward and have fun! **—Anne, Sturgis, MI**

I put tape over my mouth with a smile drawn on when I'm having trouble speaking with kindness. **—Sarah, Spokane, WA**

"I HATE YOU!" is a statement most moms have heard at some point. For a mom who invests a lot of time and thought into parenting, it can be devastating to hear. But instead of getting defensive ("Are you kidding me? After all I do for you?!") or mad ("Go to your room!"), I quickly retort, "Not as much as I love you!" My tone changes depending on the situation. If it's a half-hearted "I hate you," I will drag out the "o" in "love": "Not as much as I looooooove you!" and it usually makes her crack a smile. In a real heated "I hate you" moment, I will look her in the eye and say it dead seriously. It usually makes her pause for a moment in her anger. It's hard to be mad at someone who is trying to convey how very much they love you.

—**Ali, Lakeville, MN**

Chapter 7

The Art of Tricking Your Kid into Self-Babysitting

So you can have time to recharge, talk to another grown-up, or just take a freakin' poop in peace

WHEN MY DAUGHTER was a baby, I found the best use for Chinese take-out condiment packets—those clear plastic pouches filled with soy sauce, duck sauce, and mustard that you get with every order but never actually consume. Mine always wound up in a kitchen drawer. Because eventually I'd put them on *some*thing, right? Wrong. What I did was put them *in* something. And that something was my daughter's toy cash register.

It all started when Sasha was almost two, and I was trying to cook dinner. She kept opening the aforementioned drawer—one that, it turned out, was not easily childproofable. I didn't keep anything dangerous in there—just spices—but still, I didn't want Sasha digging around in it and dumping paprika all over the floor or getting her fingers pinched. That kid, though, was fixated. She'd sidle up to the drawer, pull it open with a glint in her eye, and say, "Special things." She'd start rooting around, trying to get ahold of these special things that were obviously special because I would shake them into our food. Y'know, to make them more "special."

How can I make this less enticing to her? I wondered. Or at least give her a little bit of what she wants, to appease her.

That's when I spotted my collection of wax paper bags full of duck sauce, mustard, and soy sauce packets.

I gave her one.

Special things, indeed! Sasha dumped out the bag and sorted through the transparent liquid-filled packets. (Good thing the casings on those things are unnaturally durable!) Attention successfully diverted. Sasha shook the packets one at a time, made piles with them—and when I took a break from the stove and sat down with her, she loaded them methodically in and out of the opening in my lap. She did get a little bummed when I had to stand up again to stir the pot, but I suggested that she put the packets in her cash register like play money. She thought this was a *brilliant* idea.

Sasha loved that cash register. Problem was, she was too young to handle play money. The coins were likely to wind up in her stomach; the bills she'd crinkle up into balls or tear to shreds. And so, while opening and closing the cash register was one of her favorite things in life, it was a little boring not to have anything actually in there.

Enter: Chinese condiments. They fit perfectly in the bill compartments. Eventually, she started sorting the packets by goo color, as if the yellow, orange, and brown each represented a different denomination.

Saved by duck sauce.

Duck sauce was my hero many nights. Until, eventually, it

wasn't. Freakin' babies. Always wanting to be entertained by something new.

Another thing we accidentally discovered Sasha liked was the car section of the newspaper. The Automobiles pages in the *New York Times* bought me and my husband at least ten minutes of uninterrupted reading on Sunday mornings. Or, let's be honest, time to pretend we're catching up on world events but really savoring our coffee. As she got older, Sasha came to prefer the Classifieds—mainly because she knew how to read the word "jobs." She'd scour the listings for a job that seemed good for her.

Really, though, I think the "me time" wins we need most as parents fall in the let-me-poop-in-peace category. When Sasha was a toddler, she took to punching me every time I sat down on the toilet. Later, she'd freak out unless I let her perch on the edge of the tub and watch. Even when she'd give in and agree to sit outside the bathroom, she'd be talking to me nonstop—alternately banging on the door and peeking. At six years old, when she herself began insisting on no people, no noise, and nothing lying on the floor when she was going number two, she did not afford me the same luxury. When Mom's on the toilet, Sasha seems to think it's the perfect time to yell that she needs a snack. Which, by the way, she is totally capable of fetching herself.

One day when she was seven, I was determined to have an uninterrupted poop. I sat her on the couch with a three-stringed guitar in open tuning and I told her, "By the time I'm off the toilet, I want you to have written a song. And when I come down, you're gonna perform it for me."

"Okay," she said, plucking at the strings.

"And it better be good," I warned.

I went upstairs and had the most peaceful poop I'd had in

years while Sasha was awake and at home. And when I came back, Sasha delivered. She yelled, "Let's get this party started," gave the guitar an enthusiastic strum, and launched into this song:

There was a man who liked to jiddi-i-o
And when he jiddi-i-o'd he liked to juggle snow

Surprisingly on key, Sasha continued to sing the saga of the man who, apparently, *really* liked to jiddi-i-o. And, according to the lyrics, did so until he died.

I have no clue what jiddi-i-o-ing is. Or what Sasha even thought it was. But I like to imagine it's the equivalent of "me time." Cooking, reading, showering, pooping, or just plain zoning out. All the stuff that, as parents, we get to savor here and there—in those rare moments when we become mad geniuses and trick our kids into occupying themselves.

Time Is a Social Construct, Right?

My children, ages four and five, nap or have quiet time every day from 1:00 p.m. to 3:00 p.m. I bought each of them an inexpensive digital clock. I've taught each not to come out of his or her room until there is a 3:00 on the clock. The win: If we are out and about and come home later, I simply reset each clock to 1:00. The point is, I need two hours of quiet time in my own house every day. (So do the children, of course.) This has been successful for a year now, since the youngest was three years old.

—Bess, Sullivan's Island, SC

My mum had a weird parenting win to get me to go to sleep. Before the days of reading the time on your iPad or phone, she would turn the clocks in our house forward by four hours. So at 7:00 p.m., all the clocks in our house would say it was 11:00 p.m. I would feel so grown-up for staying up "soooo late" and would happily go to bed. Little did I know that I wasn't even up past my normal bedtime! I was shocked when she told me years later that she did this a few times a week for five years! I'll definitely use this one on my own kids. **—Kirsty, Edinburgh, Scotland**

One New Year's Eve, we told our kids, who were four and six, they could ring in the New Year with us. They were beyond excited to be allowed to stay up so far past their regular bedtime. But we kept pushing the clocks ahead all day, so what they thought was midnight was actually 8:30. As the clock struck "12," we all went outside, whooped it up, made noise banging on pots and pans, and yelled "Happy New Year!" Then the kids went to bed by 9:00 p.m., both saying how tired they were from staying up so late. Win for the kiddos, win for Mom and Dad! **—Pam, Northport, NY**

Catching Some Extra Z's

When my sister and I were little, our parents would sometimes set up breakfast in our room for us. After we fell asleep, they would set up a small table with bowls, cereal, juice, milk (in a carton on ice), and a note telling us to make ourselves breakfast.

We would wake up in the morning and be delighted by the surprise! It felt so grown-up to make our own breakfast, but of course I've since learned that my parents did it so that we would let them sleep in a little longer, too.

—Sarah, New York, NY

When we first transitioned our daughter to a big-kid bed, she started waking up a full hour earlier. So my husband and I would take turns leading her back into her room and then playing Sleepover. He or I would sleep in her bed while she played quietly, "preparing us breakfast" and feeding it to her stuffed animals, or "reading the paper" in her room until we woke up. After about a month, she started sleeping in to her normal time. —Elizabeth, Seattle, WA

I'm a deliberately single mom. When my little one wakes up early, and I'm not ready to get out of bed, I help him down from the bed, and he has free reign in my room until I'm awake. One morning, once I was up, I was slightly mortified to realize my fourteen-month-old had been playing with my penis-shaped dildo and vibrator. Hopefully, this is just one piece of teaching him to be sex positive from the beginning?!

—Melissa, Baltimore, MD

This win is my dad's. When he was raising four teenagers and young twentysomethings, he used to go to bed early while the teens continued to watch TV. He'd ask us to keep the volume down (because of our small house), but we never did. As soon as he was in bed, we'd turn the volume back up again . . . and he'd have to come out and ask again and again . . . getting angrier each time. Finally, he realized that the breaker box for the house was located in his bedroom, and he'd simply turn off the electricity in that part of the house and go to bed! I think he only did it once or twice, and after that, the TV was always very quiet. —SARAH, FLOURTOWN, PA

Recharging

I keep a tube of glow sticks from the $1 bin at Target on hand. I have three small boys, too small to safely bathe alone. So after a bad day, I sometimes put all three boys in the tub, add the (intact) glow sticks, turn off the light, put on my headlamp, and sit on the floor of the bathroom and flip through a magazine with a glass of wine for thirty minutes.

—KEISHA, LOS ALAMOS, NM

My Lazy Dad Tip: Get your kid a fire hat and let them bury you in couch cushions. Then start screaming for help and let the firefighter rescue you. You basically just get to lay there for fifteen minutes. —JOE, ANN ARBOR, MI

One of my favorite games to play growing up was a game my dad invented and called Spy Club.

My dad would take a nap on the couch, and my brother and I would sneak around and place toys and kitchen tools on him without waking him. After about fifteen or twenty minutes, he would wake up and grade us on how effective our "spying" skills were. —CAITLIN, ALAMEDA, CA

Parenting is hardest when you're sick and just need to lie down, but you have a toddler who hasn't yet developed empathy and independence. My solution is to come up with games that require me to lie still with my eyes closed. My personal favorite is What's on My Butt?, which involves the kid finding household objects and putting them on my butt while I lie facedown on the couch. I then have to close my eyes and guess what's on my butt. It's a hit: Kids love saying "butt," and I love naps.

—**Maggie, Lynchburg, VA**

Recently, I caught my husband sitting by himself among our one-year-old daughter's toys, playing and having the time of his life. Confused, I kept watching. After a few minutes, our clingy and grumpy girl made her way over to play with him. A few more minutes, and he subtly distanced himself until eventually she was just playing on her own! A bait and switch of sorts? —**Carey, Hardwick, VT**

When my two-and-a-half-year-old is tired but doesn't want to take a nap, we read a couple of books (our normal routine) and then I read out loud to him from one of my magazines, like

Southern Living or *Bon Appétit*. To him, the articles are boring enough that he's not really interested, and I use a quiet soothing voice, so it usually takes only one or two pages for him to fall asleep. And I get to fit in reading one of my many magazines that usually just pile up. **—Bria, Atlanta, GA**

I give my eighteen-month-old daughter Post-it notes and send her on missions to put them on walls and doors and objects. It buys me time to write emails. **—Lee, Skopje, Macedonia**

When I was a kid, my mom's best friend would tell us she'd dropped a dollar in the yard and if we found it, we could keep it. My sister and I always fell for it and it felt like we spent hours searching! **—Jen, Phoenix, AZ**

When my kids hassle me while I'm trying to do something (or nothing, even), I ask them to find me the red ball. I tell them it's really important.

We don't own a red ball, but they go looking. They get distracted and I get five minutes all to myself.

—Ann, Millersville, MD

This is my mom's win; all credit goes to her. When I was a kid and Harry Potter was all the rage, not reading the books as soon as they came out was a fatal social faux pas. My brother and I couldn't risk waiting until the library finally got a copy, only for the waitlist to become interminable. However, my family didn't have a lot of money and spending on "wants" rather than "needs" was strictly off-limits. Instead, my mom would buy each new Harry Potter book right when it came out and give us three weeks to finish it before the window to return the book expired (while keeping it in pristine condition, mind you). And because neither my brother nor I was willing to read the book second, my mom bought herself days of peace and quiet while he and I sat side by side on the couch, with the book spread across both our laps as we furiously speed-read the book together. Those are some of my fondest memories with my brother, but it wasn't until recently that I understood the levels of my mom's parenting genius. There wasn't a lot of room for whimsy and indulgence on such a shoestring budget, but she still found a way to give in to our demands, encourage us to value books, and buy herself some quiet time.

—Juliana, Queens, NY

The Target Christmas catalog came in the mail today. My kid spent an hour busily circling all of the toys he liked.

—Erin, Livermore, CA

When I need a few minutes to myself, I give my three-year-old a travel-size spray bottle of water, a washcloth, and an important job to do—like cleaning her booster seat, a toy, or a window. She gets really into it and will "clean" it over and over until her spray bottle is empty! **—Bethany, Nashville, TN**

My five-year-old daughter *hates* our Roomba/iRobot vacuum. So to get her to spend time in her room, I'll tell her I need to clean, turn the Roomba on, and watch her go scampering to her room and shut the door. Then I sit back with a cup of coffee and enjoy some silence. (It also works for making her clean her toys up! I tell her to make her room "Roomba ready" and set a timer. She's *very* motivated to save her toys from being sucked into the "robot vacuum"—not that they would actually fit, but we don't tell her that!) **—Lauren, Atlanta, GA**

I do yoga during my toddler's bath. It turns out that the space in front of the tub is yoga-mat-size, and after a quick scrub-down my daughter can play independently while I squeeze in some exercise. **—Stephanie, La Mesa, CA**

My daughter has always loved playing with small packages of "things." Opening individual Band-Aids, playing with marbles or paper clips in a box, going through our junk drawers.

She once found in my purse a supply of sanitary napkins and went to town opening each package, playing with the stickers and the pads, sticking the pads on the wall and on her clothing. This kept her focus for so long, I was amazed. She's now three and still loves this activity! This morning I found she had opened six pads, laid them out on the floor in her bedroom like train cars, and placed her animals on them. "They're going on a trip!" **—Yaffa, New York, NY**

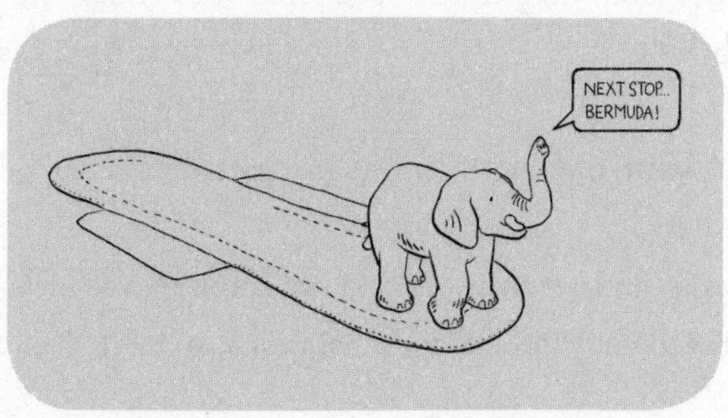

When we were kids, our mom would give us cookie trays with a cool, clear gel to finger paint. It occupied us for hours, and then she would just wash off the tray. Later, I learned it was K-Y jelly. —**Miriam, Humboldt, CA**

Talking to Other Grown-Ups in More Than Thirty-Second Spurts

On a Sunday morning, my husband and I announced to our children that we were all going to clean the house that day. Our children quietly disappeared; we did not see or hear from them for hours. Now when my husband and I want some alone time, we tell our girls it's time to clean the house. We can keep this going for a whole day—whenever they appear, we say, "Oh, are you ready to clean your room now?" (They are five and seven. We started this about a year ago, when they were past the age that not hearing from them meant we would find glitter all over the house.) —**Carolyn, Boulder, CO**

When we are entertaining in the evening on our patio, I'll pass out mini flashlights to the kiddos. They love to play Spy and can keep themselves entertained for a good while! The adults get a bit more time to socialize or to simply watch the "Spy Show." —**Leila, San Jose, CA**

My four-year-old, bless him, does not care for me to talk with other adults.

So one time, when I was midway through one of my sparkling anecdotes, I took his protestations to heart: "Oh, maybe we should talk instead about what your class is like and who your friends are? Who's your favorite classmate?"

As a relatively shy child, he opted for running off and doing something more interesting instead.

I finished my anecdote, my friends were impressed, and I felt like I was on top of the world as I gazed around at their impressed faces. **—Dave, Washington, DC**

When my husband was three or four, to occupy him and get him to play by himself, his mother gave him a saltshaker and told him that birds can't fly if you put salt on their tail. He was occupied for an hour at a time, chasing birds around the yard with a saltshaker. **—Liz, Iowa City, IA**

Just Let Me Freakin' Poop in Peace! (Or Shower, at Least?)

I keep an old toothbrush in the shower to quickly scrub little mildew spots I see when I'm in there—because who has time to clean a shower with a toddler in the house and freelance work to do during nap time? When my two-year-old daughter showers with me, I keep her busy while I'm doing my thing by letting her play with the toothbrush and a cup of water, which in turn lets me wash my hair and shave my legs (almost) uninterrupted while she is simultaneously spot cleaning my shower! I point out the spots that need scrubbing and she gets right to work—it's a nice parenting win after a long day.

—Heather, Valley Springs, CA

When my son started walking, it became more difficult for me to use the bathroom in public without him touching icky surfaces, peeking under stalls, or wandering off. I invented a game where I hand him one square of toilet paper that he gets to toss into the toilet when I'm done with my business. He patiently stands by the pot for his moment, and I am saved from having to stop midstream to chase him down. Now, almost a year later, he loves it so much that he eagerly runs into our home bathrooms for the game, too.

—Maureen, Presque Isle, ME

If you wrap your toddler's forgotten toys in aluminum foil, they turn into exciting "presents" that are the perfect amount of challenge to open. This will buy you enough time to read a short article, eat a granola bar, or go to the bathroom!

—Becca, Minneapolis, MN

If my beloved toddler sensed I was heading to the toilet, he was right on my tail. I've never been good at "going" with an audience. Stuff, literally, of nightmares. So one day, with my little companion on my heels and complaining as I shut the door, I asked him to go choose me a teddy and to choose a really special one. He was a slow mover at that time, so it gave me all the time I needed to commune with nature. Of course, he quickly learned to move a whole lot faster. So as I was heading to the loo, he'd pretty much beat me to the door, having raced to fetch me the teddy I clearly needed to get the business done. This went on for a year or two. Backfire! (Pun intended.)

—Gretchen, Sydney, Australia

I just needed a few minutes alone to do things after work like use the toilet or—gasp!—take a minute to touch up my manicure/pedicure, and my one-year-old was not having it. My parenting win? I would give him a roll of toilet paper and allow him to go to town TPing my bedroom. It would buy me five to ten minutes of time to myself. The upside? I was usually able to reroll most of it back onto the roll for decorating use later. Oh, and buying in bulk helped, too.

—Laura, Willow Grove, PA

My bathroom win: I'd open the cabinet and hand my one-year-old a box of tampons. She loved taking them out and putting them back in. It kept her happily entertained and I got a few minutes to sit on the toilet alone.

—Sarah, Durham, NC

Needing to take a shower, I learned I could play peekaboo with the curtain. Now my shower is my son's favorite part of the day! **—Dawn, Montreal, QC, Canada**

Chapter 8

The Art of Making This Scary-Ass World Less Scary

Because real things are often scarier than imaginary things

When Sasha was four years old, she learned the story of Martin Luther King Jr. I mean, she'd heard it before in school and from me and her dad. But this time the teacher read a book that went all the way through to the end. That night, Sasha was screaming uncontrollably and I couldn't figure out why. Finally, after wrapping my arms around her to try to help her control her fit, she shouted, "You lied about Martin Luther King!"

"What do you mean?" I asked.

"You said he just died," she said accusingly. "He didn't just die. He was shot with a gun."

"Oh," I said. "You're right. It's very, very upsetting, but that's true."

She continued her tirade through tears: "He was the best person in the world. He had the best ideas. And they killed him."

Sasha hasn't ever personally known anyone who's died. But

after hearing the MLK story, she got it in her head that if someone like him could be shot dead, so could I. So could her dad.

So could she.

No amount of consoling would help. She screamed at the top of her lungs several nights in a row. I went to the teacher and asked if she'd consider revisiting the story and help the children process their new knowledge about the assassination of one of our country's greatest heroes. Maybe assure them that they were safe. Maybe acknowledge that it was a scary and awful thing, but that King's words and actions have had a lasting impact on our society. And that there is more work to be done, but the movement he led has had a far reach.

The teacher told me none of the other kids had a problem hearing about the assassination, and this was Sasha's issue. I'm not sure how she figured Sasha was the only four-year-old in her class to take the news hard; if I hadn't said anything to her, she wouldn't have even known that Sasha was freaked out. In any case, the teacher told me the class had moved on to other subjects. The MLK unit was over.

But Sasha's fear of death was not.

Every morning on the way to school I was assaulted with a new barrage of questions about death: How am I going to die? How are *you* going to die? When are you going to die? How old will I be when you die? How many ways are there to die?

"I don't know," I'd say. "It's really impossible to know."

"Let's count," she'd say. "Getting shot, old age, being hit by a truck, drowning . . ."

As Sasha's fear of death deepened, so did my fear of getting in the car with her. Some people wake up to their morning coffee; I'd wake up to my morning imagining-of-my-own-death.

Eventually the intensity of Sasha's death probe did diminish. My guess is, it had a lot to do with entering kindergarten and riding the bus. Surrounded by other children each morning on the way to school, she had plenty of things to focus on other than her own mother's demise.

Still, though, her death questions will hit me when I'm least expecting them.

We'll be playing school. She's the teacher; I'm the student. And she'll say, "Arthur had five teachers. Two of them died. How many teachers does Arthur have left?"

I'll go, "*Sasha.*"

She'll go, "Do the math."

Or I'll be snuggling with her on the couch, stroking her head, and she'll ask me sweetly, "How do they get your body in the ground?" Then she'll want to know how they turn your body to coal (cremation). And what can you do if you don't want to become coal?

Death is scary. Maybe the scariest thing of all. I just wish I was better equipped to help her little inquisitive mind worry about it less. Especially when it's something that freaks me out, too.

Sasha herself figured out the win that helps calm her down about death—at least in the short term.

At bedtime, she'll get dressed in her skeleton pj's—black fabric, with bones that glow in the dark. Then she'll slip on all ten of her glow-in-the-dark monster fingers and her glow-in-the-dark vampire teeth. Next, she'll stand under the bulb in her closet. Once she thinks her glow stuff is glowy enough, she'll shut off the lights.

That's when she's ready to kill me.

She'll come after me—bones, teeth, fingers aglow, shout-whispering, "I'm going to get you, Mommy. I'm going to put you in jail for ten hundred days."

I play the damsel in distress: "What?! Ten hundred days! I can't survive ten hundred days!"

"Then you'll *die,*" she says creepily in my ear.

Cue: me doing my best over-the-top horror movie–style death scene.

We might do this three times in one sitting. It'd be more if it were up to her, but that's about as much dying as I can manage in a night.

While death has definitely been Sasha's biggest fear, it's not her only one. Another thing high on her list is dogs. Maybe this is because when she was five, my cousin's golden Lab, Romeo, ran at her with a kitchen knife in his mouth. For real. He grabbed it off a counter by the handle, blade pointed straight ahead, and charged right at my kiddo. Luckily, my husband jumped in front of her just in time and somehow stopped Romeo without getting stabbed. Prior to that, Sasha had been nervous around Romeo, and we'd been telling her he was a friendly dog and he wouldn't hurt her if she was gentle with him. Little did we know, running around with a knife was his "favorite thing"—according to my cousin.

After the knife incident, Sasha's fear of dogs multiplied. She'd recoil in tears at the sight of the white fluffy terriers that go for a walk around our block every morning.

Sasha started drawing dogs obsessively. Sometimes it'd be a girl walking a dog; sometimes it was just a dog on its own. Usually it was a sunny day, with a smattering of raindrops—so you can have a rainbow, of course. The dogs got more and more detailed. They had shoes with shoelaces. Fancy sweaters. Claws. Eyelashes.

These days, when you ask Sasha her favorite animal, she'll say "dog." Though I still don't think I've ever seen her pet one.

Drawing has become one of Sasha's go-to coping mechanisms for her fears. She filled a whole notepad with pictures of poo back when she was withholding. And when we saw a girl bang her face on a metal bar at the playground and lose a tooth, Sasha drew that, too. She used a lot of red marker on that one, for the blood. (I hope the Bloody Fairy didn't pay that girl a visit.)

I sometimes wonder if Sasha got the drawing-your-fears idea from a book I made with her, telling the story of what happened when she broke her leg going down the slide. At a year and a half, she was too young to write words, so I'd write down each step of the story on a page, read it to her, and she'd draw how she felt with Cray-Pas. It was remarkable how she really made the scary parts look scary by drawing with more pressure.

Sometimes two dimensions is not enough, and Sasha likes to be able to hold the object of her fear in her hands.

The first time my husband and I spent a weekend away from her, she was two years old. We'd left her with my parents in Connecticut while we drove to Cape Cod and spent a few days there in the chilly spring.

I didn't expect that a couple of nights away would have much impact on Sasha. She loved spending time with my folks and tinkering in my mom's art studio. But when we came back to pick her up, she refused to look at me.

Luckily, though, my mom sent her home with a souvenir. A clay sculpture Sasha had made during her visit. It was an insect-type creature encrusted with buttons and beads and cut-up pieces of fluorescent bendy straws.

Its title: *Cape Cod.*

Fear of Needles

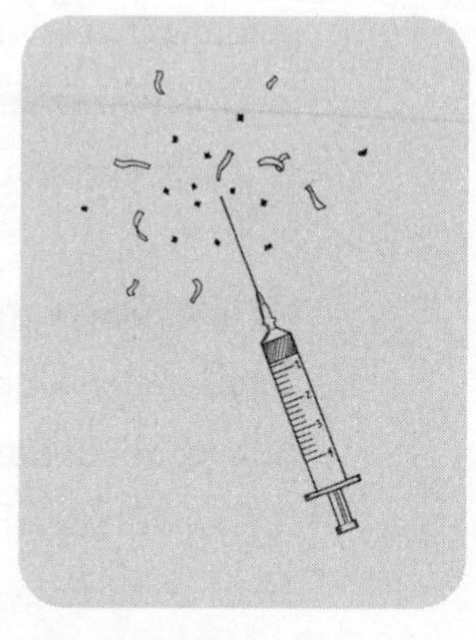

My daughter, age four, had to go to the hospital to get some blood drawn. She'd had needles before and always hated them—it usually ended with me and two nurses holding her down while a third nurse handled the needle.

This time, though, we talked about it in the morning at home to prepare. We talked about all the things at the hospital that don't hurt and how drawing blood would only last a second. Then I asked if she wanted to choose a soft toy or book to bring. She chose a few things, then found a paper-cone birthday hat and put it on. Somehow that was her superpower—not only did it make her feel better, but *everyone* at the hospital, including staff and patients, had a big smile for her because they thought it was her birthday. We made it through the needle with no tears! **—Abigale, Fergus, ON, Canada**

My six-year-old used to take vaccine shots like a champ, but now she is very afraid. She will scream and cry and throw a big fit if she knows she has to get a shot. Most recently, she had to get a flu shot and I didn't know what I was going to do. She likes to draw and write, so I came up with the idea of writing a story in her notebook about a girl who had to fight the flu dragon.

She wrote about the flu dragon that breathed fire on the girl and gave her fevers and made her feel very sick. The girl had a pointy sword (needle) with magic potion inside and poked the flu dragon and *poof*! The flu dragon disappeared! She got so into the story that we created a homemade, glittery "vaccine sword" and we marched all the way to the doctor's office and got into character. She took her vaccine with minimal tears and was very brave. Phew! Now I have a "vaccine sword" that she can hold onto for future shots. **—Thaomy, San Francisco, CA**

My eleven-year-old daughter had a very scary and painful autoimmune illness that started a week before her seventh birthday (Guillain-Barre syndrome). Her immune system attacked the myelin sheath surrounding her spinal cord and caused her to become partially paralyzed—and lose her ability to walk, move her limbs, smile, and cough. She was hospitalized, treated, and made a full recovery within a year of her illness.

Despite having experienced incredible nerve pain and weight loss, and the inability to be touched or move without pain, her lasting fear is of needles. She is terrified of shots to the point of panic attacks, hiding behind the exam table and hyperventilating. Her fear has developed into a phobia.

Once, after I took her to get immunizations and had to have two nurses and myself hold her down to get immunized, my husband—her dad—came up with a win. He is in emergency medicine and decided to teach her how to give him a shot. He started out by giving himself a shot of saline in front of her several times. Then she held and touched the needle. A huge breakthrough recently is that she was able to give him a shot and thought it was kind of fun. Her long-term goal is to be able to give herself a shot.

I am so grateful that my husband has the knowledge and capability to help her through this. Hopefully she will be able to have routine blood draws and immunizations in her future and, more important, feel confident that she can overcome her fears. —Emily, Minneapolis, MN

Fear of Trying New Things

My daughter was taking swimming lessons and wouldn't put her head underwater. The swim coach suggested that I leave, which sounded like counterintuitive advice, but I did, and she finally made progress in my absence. A year later, I used his advice again when it was time for her to get dental X-rays. She'd refused previously, so when her appointment rolled around, I told the receptionist I wasn't planning to come back with my daughter and why. She told the hygienist, while I sold my daughter on this new "big girl" milestone. Of course, she got the X-rays with no problem. Thanks, swim coach!

—Jennifer, Madison, WI

My daughter can be very fearful of trying new physical activities, like riding a bike or ice-skating, because she is afraid of getting hurt. At the same time, she has recently become interested in her ancestors (thank you, *Moana*!) and we have traced her matrilineal line back a few generations. I printed photos of her grandmother, great-grandmother, and great-great-grandmother, and we talked about the family tree.

Recently, she fell on her bike while learning to ride and didn't want to get back up for fear of getting hurt. I told her to "draw on the power of her ancestors" to find strength and bravery to get back on her bike again. I then dramatically called out the names of her ancestors as they related to her. "You are Zelda, Daughter of Betty, Granddaughter of Marie, Great-Granddaughter of Lucile, Great-Great-Granddaughter of Lucile, Great-Great-Great-Granddaughter of Nellie, Great-Great-Great-Great-Granddaughter of Jane!" I got about three generations in and she hopped back up on her bike and was bravely coasting down the hill as I called out the rest.

—Betty, Modesto, CA

My nine-year-old daughter is a perfectionist and can get anxious about new situations and what will be expected from her. I have developed the First Pancake Philosophy, which really helps her deal with the uncertainty and potential failure of new experiences, like her first dance exam or first sports game.

When you make pancakes, you know that the first pancake is not going to be a good one. It's the pancake where you are checking if the pan is the right temperature, how long to wait to flip it, and whether the batter is the right consistency. It's the trial pancake. (It's also the one the cook gets to eat!)

So we say that the first time you do anything—like play your first sports game of the season—that's the first pancake. Of course, you will be a little uncertain and make mistakes. But they're to be expected and you get to learn from them for the next game.

Likewise with her dance exam. We got there early so she could do quite a few run-throughs of her routine and get that "first pancake" dance out of the way.

I've often tried to talk about learning from mistakes, but it's never got through to her as clearly as using the pancake analogy. Now, mistakes that might have put her into a tailspin she just shrugs off as "that was the first pancake."

—**Jane, Dunedin, New Zealand**

As a small child, I was extremely shy and had very little self-confidence. It was a problem because, when confronted with another child who would annoy me, I would simply remain silent. At kindergarten, even though I loved my teacher, I was scared of being asked questions. I was also scared of loneliness and of being without my parents. I even refused to stay overnight at my grandparents'.

My parents realized this rather quickly and wanted to improve my self-confidence. The solution for them: Let's make her sing in a choir and on a stage. I was five years old. Apparently, they realized that I liked singing and I joined a carol-singing choir. Later, I was selected to sing solo onstage and on TV. It seems to have worked—being in a choir gave me the confidence to mingle with other kids. By age seven or eight, I was traveling with the choir, even without my parents. It wasn't about fame or anything; this was in the 1980s in Belgium. Child stars were not a thing and there is no way my parents wanted that. It was just a hobby that would allow me to get rid of some fears. —**Marie, Montreal, QC, Canada**

We moved to a new state and my son was nervous about his first day at his new school. I made a big production of finding a "very special lucky penny" that I'd saved and only use "when I really need good luck" . . . and then presented it to him, saying he could rub it throughout the day when he was really nervous (like lunchtime!) for good luck. He came home that afternoon and was grinning ear to ear. He excitedly told me, "That penny was so lucky! I made friends!" And then handed it back to me, saying he wouldn't need it again. **—Klarysa, Roswell, GA**

You learn to ride a bike by falling down fifty times. When my girls were learning to ride, that is what I told them. I showed them the how-to part, then left them to practice. We had a big, safe, paved area next to our house. I remember being in the kitchen when my five-year-old daughter came running in for a drink of water, panting, and shouted, "Twelve!" . . . then ran back out to keep going. Every time they fell, instead of viewing it as a failure, they were one step closer to riding. Neither reached thirty falls before they could ride.

—Chip, Baton Rouge, LA

Until the age of about seven, my son was terrified of making a mistake or failing. He had always been hard on himself, but this came to a head when he tried playing Little League baseball for the first time. Suddenly, every strikeout was another opportunity to berate himself. I came up with the idea for what I called a Confidence Binder. I wrote a poem that centered on his loved ones, as well as sports heroes, and the mistakes they make on a daily basis, and I kept this poem at the front of the binder to be read together each night. After reading the poem, we worked on completing a chart that I created. My son would have to write down three things that he did right or that made him proud throughout the day. Then he wrote down one mistake he made—something that he wished had gone differently. We talked about how to improve next time something like this happened. Then we ended by discussing the fact that there are almost always going to be more positive things each day, because of the wonderful person that he was (and still is), as evidenced in the chart. My son is now twelve, and while he still tends to be hard on himself, as many high achievers are, he is no longer afraid of making a mistake.

—Farrah, Middlesex, NJ

Fear of Animals

My neighborhood in Portland has two main daytime animals: crows and squirrels. I think of fall here as the season of "crows vs. squirrels" because of how entertaining it is to watch them vying for walnuts. So crows and squirrels were the animals my kids were first delighted by, watching them from the windows. When my twins were two, the crows had their babies and these enormous child-crows would sit on the sidewalks and in the grass, squawking for food. Which is, I think, how my daughter's fear of birds started. It got so bad that if she heard birds singing, she would launch into my arms and say, "Mama, I don't like a bird. Take me inside!" Going outdoors became terrifying, and outside is really the only place mamas of two-year-olds get a break.

Soon she was afraid of all animals—except our dogs, Crawdad and Artemis. When asked what animals she liked, her response was "food." We were pretty stumped by what seemed like a weird phobia for a toddler. We decided to create one positive bird experience for her daily. I invited my mom, an avid birdwatcher, to bring a bird book over, and together they put stickers in the margins. We got my daughter a pink flamingo shirt (she loved it but also insisted that flamingos were not birds). We talked about mama and baby birds, we found bird finger puppets, we did the chicken dance, we called to each other using bird sounds.

Well, she still answers no when asked if she likes birds, but she will now happily go outside and play. Phew.

—Anna, Portland, OR

We live out in the country, and when my daughter was four, we had an aggressive rooster in our flock of chickens. He'd sort of charged us before, but if you pretended like you were going to kick him, he'd back off. My daughter was scared of him, so my husband taught her that if he came at her, to wave her stick at him and yell, "Go away, rooster!"

One day she was in the front yard playing, and I had ducked into the house for a second. I heard her shouting at the rooster, and then I just heard screaming, so I ran out to see that bastard rooster on her back, and she was trying to run up the porch steps. I ran and grabbed her and pulled her into the house and slammed the door. I just hugged her and we both sobbed for a long time; it was so scary. I mean, she had tried so bravely to do what her dad had taught her, and it didn't work. Gah, it makes me cry just thinking about it.

Then I texted my husband, who was at his grandparents' farm down the road, to come and kill that fucking rooster *now*.

So he came and, like a good farm boy, got his rifle out and shot it. By then, my daughter and I had calmed down, but we were still really shaky feeling. And here's where we get to the weird parenting win part. My husband knew my daughter liked to collect feathers, so he brought the dead rooster to her and showed her how to pluck feathers from it, and she got totally into it and was all about getting these pretty feathers to add to her collection. She could see for herself that the rooster would never hurt her again, *plus* she got pretty, iridescent feathers out of the deal. It was such a primal way of declaring victory over this horrible creature, and I was not sure it was the best plan, but it worked. **—Nina, Cedarville, AR**

I don't know where it came from, but my four-year-old daughter is terrified of lobsters. She has nightmares about lobsters somewhat frequently. My husband went in one time when she was crying in the middle of the night, and she said, "I had a dream that a lobster ate Grandpa!" Now we have to spray her room with "lobster spray" every night before bed to keep the lobsters away. **—Bethany, Vienna, VA**

I raised three spirited, beautiful daughters (including twins) to adulthood as a single working mother. We lived in a house about an hour outside of Vancouver, British Columbia, in Canada. The house was big enough for all of us, with lots of lawn, trees, and farms nearby. There was one drawback: *wolf spiders*. These large, ugly, hairy beasts are harmless, but they are more than cringeworthy and struck terror into my girls.

The situation always got worse when the weather got colder. This meant the spiders would start finding their way into the house. The spider-checking-destroying job I had to undertake each and every evening at bedtime was overwhelming and seemed endless. In order to calm three nearly hysterical, overtired youngsters, I made up a new, universal spider rule, which was: Spiders are afraid of perfume and won't go near the stuff. I sprayed perfume in all the corners, windows, and across the threshold of their doors. To my relief, the girls bought it, and bedtime became simple, with a spritz here and there of my least favorite scent. I used this method for many seasons while the girls grew, and it bought me hours of blissful silence and evening serenity.

Fast-forward to a year or so ago and a conversation I was having with the girls on spiders and how to keep them from invading a bedroom. Calmly, my oldest daughter told me that she still uses the foolproof method of perfume deterrence, as if it were scientific fact. After all, it had worked all those years in the house. I had to come clean with them. I told them that I had invented the whole thing in an effort to simply *get them to sleep after a long day*. They were shocked and confused. How could I have done this?! I gave it a while to sink in, and then they saw the next-to-impossible parenting situation I faced at bedtime and eventually applauded me for my ingenuity. To this day, we still talk about the "perfume solution" and how it saved my sanity and made everyone's lives run a little smoother. **—Maria, Chilliwack, BC, Canada**

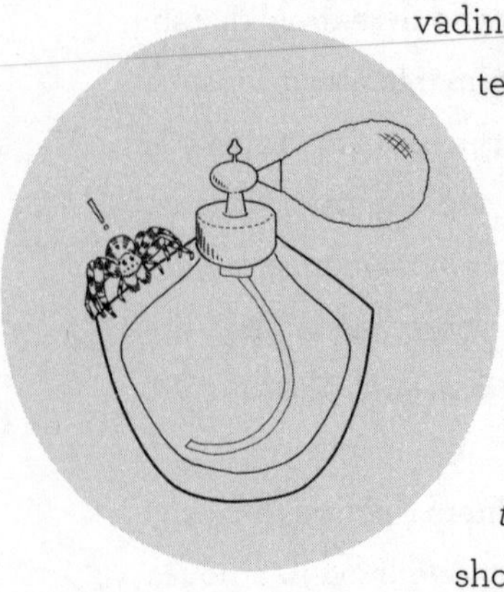

Fear of Death

After answering my four-year-old for the one hundredth time about "Why do people have to die?" I lost it. I started making outrageous statements like, "People die because they try to see how many poison toadstools they can eat. People die because they try to take a bath and blow-dry their hair at the same time. People die because they try and count how many teeth a great white shark has in its mouth. People die because they try to juggle baby cobras." He thought this was very funny. Best of all, he stopped asking me why people die.

—Karina, Montclair, NJ

When I was about five, I became really afraid of death. I was afraid that I would die and that my parents and my grandparents and my friends would die. This fear became worse at night, when I was trying to fall asleep. At first my parents tried to calm me by saying it wouldn't happen for a long time and I had nothing to worry about. That did not help at all. Then my dad explained to me that if people did not die, the Earth would become overcrowded and people would run out of natural resources and would have to eat each other. Somehow this made sense to me and death became a reasonable outcome instead of a scary one. **—Olga, Vinnitsa, Ukraine**

Not long after a group of firemen visited my four-year-old's preschool, she became outrageously terrified of fires. We're talking nightmares about being burned alive, getting trapped in smoky buildings, not being able to find her family after escaping the embers of our home . . . the works! Despite my best efforts to calm her nerves by reassuring her that fires almost never happen in people's homes and that we're very careful and keep the smoke detectors in good working order, her fears persisted. That is, until I thought of a way to build a positive association with fires.

One night after dinner, we went out back with a bag of marshmallows, two chocolate bars, and a box of graham crackers, and my daughter instantly knew what we were doing. I handed her a marshmallow on the end of a long skewer and showed her how to hold it over the fire. She was hesitant at first, but after seeing me and her big sister roast our marshmallows to perfection, then craft our s'mores, she wanted to get in on it!

We talked about how the fire doesn't move all by itself (her biggest fear). And even when our marshmallows caught on fire, we just blew them out and kept toasting. That night, we used the campfire sound on her noise machine while she slept, and we talked about dreaming of making and eating s'mores. Oddly enough, that experience making treats over an open fire seemed to do the trick. No more fire nightmares for us!

—Evie, Houston, TX

My daughter often experiences fears that come up right before bedtime, when she is processing scary news she has heard about recently—like a mass shooting. I was the same way when I was young. I remember the end of the day being the scariest time of the day for me. As an adult, I learned how to manage random fears before bed and make myself calm enough to go to sleep quickly and happily. What I taught myself, and then my daughter, is not to hide from the scary thoughts. Let them be present in your head and fill your mind with them, but imagine them being a sheet of paper that you crumple into a ball. With each new scary thought, or part of the scary story, add a crumpled sheet of paper to your ball. When all the scary thoughts are out of your head and in the ball, take your foot and pretend to be a striker hitting a soccer ball into the goal. This is her favorite part. We take the imaginary ball and do a huge kick out into the universe across her bed. She says it goes to the giant Dumpster in the sky far, far away in a different galaxy, never to be seen again. Once we have kicked the ball away, we then fill our heads with good thoughts, which often include Lisa Frank unicorns, playing in the sunshine, my daughter's birthday, and seeing friends. We do it about twice a week and call it "kicking out the bad thoughts."

—Margaritte, Tulsa, OK

My dad was a mortician—technically a teacher of the mortuary sciences, as he taught and wrote textbooks rather than practiced. So when it came to being afraid of death—and dealing with my fear of death—his tactic was to put on his mortician cap and be completely clinical about it. At funerals of close family members, for instance, his answer to our coffin-side weeping, and to my fear when it was time to go and kiss the corpse, was to comment on what kind of job the funeral home did with dressing the body—whether or not he approved of the makeup on the face of the person who was my grandmother . . . that kind of thing. My initial reaction was basically to be horrified at what he was saying, to feel like he was being cold and creepy and unfeeling. But later, I think I began to take a weird kind of comfort in the distance and distraction of thinking about post-mortem makeup techniques and hair arrangements. It was a comfort in understanding that this body that had to be powdered and posed in a way that vaguely resembled someone I knew and loved was no longer that person. That the very best work the funeral directors did behind the scenes would only ever amount to a poor imitation. And so I didn't have to be afraid of a dead body, because that's all it was.

—Amy, Washington, DC

Have you noticed how many parents die in books, fairy tales, and Disney movies? So has my inquisitive five-year-old. Whenever she asks me, "What happened? How did she die?" I always say, "She died of smallpox." Smallpox! It is not scary because it has been totally eradicated, so she has no need to worry that the same fate will befall anyone she loves.

—Jennifer, Atlanta, GA

Chapter 9

The Art of Getting Your Kid to Tell You Things

Communicating with tight-lipped kids on matters big and small

MY KID IS CONSTANTLY TALKING. She talks through car rides, through meals, through TV shows. She talks while making pretend smartphones out of paper, while brushing her teeth, while singing karaoke. She talks all day long, right up until the moment we turn off the lights and say good night. Even then, she talks as I'm walking out the door. If I ever sit quietly, say, at the dinner table, for more than ten seconds, she asks me accusingly, "Why are you not talking?" As if something is terribly wrong. Often my answer is, "I'm chewing!"

Still, for all her talking, Sasha has never been one for talking about feelings. If she's upset, she'd way rather scream.

That's starting to change, and my ears and blood pressure thank her. But back when she was in preschool, she was going through something intense. She was screaming a lot, hitting me a lot—she even bit me on the butt once. When I'd ask her to tell me what she was feeling, she'd yell, "I don't *have* any feelings!" It was hard to get to the bottom of what was troubling her. One afternoon, though, I uncovered a piece of the puzzle—in shocking detail—without even trying.

Sasha had just come home from school. We were hanging out in the living room, sitting side by side in an armchair. She was small enough that we could fit that way without feeling squished.

"Let's play school," Sasha said. "I'll be Lily and you be me." Lily was her best friend at the time.

"Okay," I said, putting on my best peppy Sasha voice. "Hi, Lily."

"You better play with me, Sasha," she said, suddenly turning snippy.

"I *am* playing with you," I said.

"No," she whispered in my ear, "say you want to go play with someone else."

Ah, we were following some script in her head. I quickly got with the program: "I want to play with Brielle."

"You can't play with her." She stuck her red-cheeked face up in mine, pausing for effect. "And if you do, you won't get the big surprise."

"What's the big surprise?" I asked.

"I'm not telling," Sasha said. "You'll only find out if you don't ever play with anyone else."

"But I want the big surpriiiiise," I fake-whined.

"Too bad," she said, sliding off the chair and stomping away. "You don't deserve it."

I didn't have to ask to know we were reenacting a real scene from the playground. It broke my heart to know Sasha was already experiencing friend drama. But I also recognized in that moment that Sasha had dropped a giant gift in my lap. Without naming a single emotion, she was forcing me to feel everything she was feeling. And when I can feel what she's feeling, it helps me have more patience when, out of the blue, she loses her little mind.

I'll Be You has become a regular part of my parenting repertoire. I'll be you; you be the teacher. I'll be you; you be our cat. Then there's the one she requests most frequently: I'll be you and you be me. It can be tough to see your kid do a spot-on imitation of you, but hey, you get to imitate them back.

My pal Kirsten, who gave me the phrase "the longest shortest time," is a child therapist, and she tells me this role-playing thing is a variation on a real therapeutic technique she uses with kids. Dolls, blocks, trucks, and stuffed animals all can become props for seeing deeply into a child's inner world. "If you have a question about how they felt about something that happened at school, pick up a stuffed animal and pretend the stuffed animal is your kid and you are the teacher who yelled at them," Kirsten says. She adds, though, that "the key to this type of play is that you can start it, but as soon as they join you, correct you, or change the story, you have to follow their lead." With kids who are reluctant to talk about their feelings, Kirsten says it can help to ask things along the way, like, "I wonder why the pig kicked the chicken?" or "How did the truck feel when it lost its wheel?"

As a therapist, Kirsten has all sorts of tricks for getting kids to talk. And she's used many of them over the years with her now adolescent son, Jack. But as Jack got older, she says there's only one trick that has worked consistently. It's a tip she actually found in a fashion magazine interview with Angelina Jolie—who, somewhere in the middle of talking about acting and her sex life with Brad Pitt, began ruminating on raising a teenager. Plus, how you spend all this time with little kids, teaching and talking, and when they hit puberty, you suddenly need to shift gears and start listening. Kirsten remembers reading this and being like, *Oh, wait, all I need to do is SHUT THE FUCK UP!*

Kirsten puts the shut-the-fuck-up technique into play a lot as a mom—but especially every spring, when Jack traditionally goes through a week or two of complete and utter pissed-off-ed-ness at everyone and everything around him. It's happened annually ever since he was in elementary school. Kirsten thinks it's a sign of an emotional growth spurt or something. Anyway, on the nights when Jack is going bonkers, Kirsten takes a walk with him. Well, "with" is a loose term. It's more like "behind." Jack walks at a tight clip, keeping a foot ahead of Kirsten, ranting about whatever's on his mind. Meanwhile, Kirsten races to keep up . . . and she listens.

As a person who processes problems with kids for a living, Kirsten says that keeping quiet in these moments is one of the most challenging things she's ever done. She feels an urgency to fix things, to solve Jack's problems, to tell him that she's gonna find that kid who hurt his feelings and punch him in the face. And on their very first walks, she'd give in to her impulse. Not the punching part; the comforting words part. But whenever she piped up, Jack would shut down. That's when she began experimenting with silence. She'd remind herself that she'd spent his entire childhood guiding him in how to express his feelings, and right now, all he needed was the space to do that. Her job was to let him vent—to let him go, go, go. Until he started repeating himself, at which point she'd gently guide him to another topic or say that it was time to head home.

After their walks, Kirsten says, Jack usually seems to feel better—less worked up. And her tongue is sore. Not from talking, but from biting it.

Games

When my son was in preschool, we made up a game called Hibernation. We would pretend to be bears and climb into bed, under our fluffy white down comforter. While in there, I found that I could ask him pretty much any question about his friends, teachers, worries, or aspirations. He's in elementary school now, and I don't know how long it'll last, but sometimes he'll even ask me if we can hibernate so he can tell me something.

—Kate, Minnetonka, MN

When I want my child to talk to me about his life, I tell him about my day. It's not really fair for him to be the only one sharing. Sometimes if I can't think of anything, I bust out Rose, Bud, Thorn (which I learned from my sister). "Rose" is the best thing about our day, "bud" is what we hope today set in motion for tomorrow, and "thorn" is the worst thing about our day.

I have found that I need to tell my child the sort of stuff I want him to tell me: who hurt my feelings, things that scared me. It's sweet because he remembers and asks me about stuff later (he's seven). I'm a high school teacher, and I had a really tough class one semester. At the same time, my child was having a hard time behaving at school. I told him about a student who had been behaving really badly, but who I talked to and had apologized for a misunderstanding. The next night, he said, "Mommy, can you tell me another story about a kid who used to be bad and now he's good?" I told him I could talk about a student I hoped would be better soon. A few weeks later, he asked, "Did you see the girl who knocked your coffee cup into the sink today? Is she better?" It turned out she was better and I had forgotten how much she had worried me at the time.

It's fun to think of stories he'll like. I told him about my ant farm at school and a student who had bitten off a piece of his apple from lunch to feed them. My child came to a school event later and met the apple kid—I didn't remember that I'd talked about him. But when I introduced them, my child said, "You're the apple kid!" Everyone was excited!

I think this would be harder if I weren't a teacher, but my child likes to know what I do all day, and it makes him feel like his life is not so big and unknown to me when I let him know I get scared and worried and hurt and happy and silly, too.

—Sara, Marietta, GA

When I was growing up, my parents would occasionally offer an "ollie-ollie-in-come-free." The rules were that we could tell them anything and we wouldn't get in trouble. We usually used these moments to confess about breaking rules. It got to the point where we felt bold enough to request an "ollie-ollie-in-come-free" when we needed to talk about something but didn't want to get in trouble. My parents learned so much that we probably wouldn't have told them otherwise.

—Kelsey, Salt Lake City, UT

My win for how to get kids to tell you about their day is to play True or False. Everyone goes around the table during dinner and tells one thing that may have happened that day and then everyone else guesses if it is true or false. For our twins, the idea that they could possibly trick their parents motivated them to share. Before we started this game, I couldn't get my kids to tell me anything about their day; this game really helped us. **—Karyn, Washington, DC**

When my kids were teenagers, I would always have a jigsaw puzzle on the dining room table. The idea was for me to be sitting at the table, working on the puzzle when they got home from school, a dance, a party, or just being out for the night. When they came in, they would stop by to say hi, and instead of going right up to their room, they always would try to find a piece to put in the puzzle. One piece led to two pieces, and before they knew it, they had sat down, continuing to "help" me. I would start to ask questions about their day or their evening out, and before long I knew what was going on in their life, whether I wanted to know it or not. I still have a *great* relationship with my boys, and they still feel comfortable talking to me, too! **—Christine, Cleveland, OH**

During my daughter Emma's preteen and teen years, I was always looking for creative ways to get her attention, spend time with her, and get her talking. It was also a struggle to get her to keep her room straightened up. I started a new game with her, which I called Clean or Dirty. We would hole up in her room for a couple of hours sorting through all the clothes on the floor, organizing, and cleaning. I would pick up each item (as she was still lying in her bed, wishing I would get the heck out of her room and let her sleep) and ask, "Clean or dirty?" Some of the most amazing, intimate, and informative conversations happened during those times—and we got her room cleaned. She is twenty-one now. We still talk about Clean or Dirty, and it always stirs up warm feelings for both of us.

—Heidi, Glendale, AZ

It was getting harder to connect with my daughter. As she got closer to her friends, she was rolling her eyes at me more and dismissing what I had to say. Then I started to hear her say things like, "I hate my (body part)" and "I am such a dummy." I knew that Mom telling her that she was lovely and great was kind of lame, so one night when it was just the two of us at dinner, I asked her what she liked about herself. She rolled her eyes a little and said, "I don't know," with a shrug.

Then I suggested we trade compliments. You tell me something you like about me and I will say something I like about you, and we would stop whenever she wanted. She went first. Something about thinking about what a good compliment for me would be ("I like that you always try to see things from other people's perspective") enabled her to really hear the compliments about her ("I like how you make your friends feel strong and connected and you bring out the best in them"). After about five, she stood up and threw her arms around me and said, "I love you, Mom." It was pretty amazing.

—Debbie, Charlotte, NC

Car Talk

My mom is a health and phys ed teacher, so she got pretty good at talking to teenagers about sex. One of her techniques, which I know I will adopt for my own kids when they reach the right age, is to start the talk while the child is in the back seat of the car.

No kid wants to sit and try (not) to make eye contact with a parent when they're hearing uncomfortable information or being asked embarrassing questions. This arrangement totally alleviates the issue. Wait until you're driving the kid to an event that they're grateful to be going to, with friends who can be used as a venting/sounding board if they need to process the information. They're stuck in the car, so they can't run away to avoid the conversation—they're forced to hear what you have to say. Plus, when you're done (hopefully right as you're arriving at your destination), they exit the vehicle and you both can forget the awkwardness that just ensued.

—Sarah, Minneapolis, MN

When I was a teenager, my mom would start difficult conversations in the car. I think there was something special about the intimate proximity and the fact that you couldn't leave. It also was helpful because you didn't actually have to look at each other but still could have a meaningful conversation. The stuff she would bring up usually centered on grades, problems I was having with friend cliques at school, and eventually sex stuff. I distinctly remember a conversation we had the summer before my senior year of high school. In the safety of the car, my mom broached the subject of whether or not my boyfriend of two years and I had discussed having sex (we had talked about it but hadn't acted on our ideas). During that car ride—in the '94 black Volvo wagon—on suburban Chicago streets, my mom and I decided it was time I go to the gynecologist and start taking the pill. Now that I have a four-year-old, I've already used the magic of the car conversations to talk about her days at preschool and her thoughts and feelings.

—Caroline, Arlington, VA

It all started with the *Titanic*. Not the Hollywood movie version starring Leonardo DiCaprio and Kate Winslet, but the real thing—the famed ocean liner that sank in the wee hours of April 15, 1912, in the black waters of the Atlantic Ocean. Audrey's biological dad, who is now in his sixties, has, since he was about Audrey's age (seven), been fascinated, preoccupied, downright obsessed with the *Titanic*—in all its glories, its shapes, its peoples and peepholes, down to the tiniest details like how many nuts and bolts were used for the windows facing the side that sank first. In his "past" life, he was a painter; he painted more than one hundred versions of the *Titanic*. The Duke Ellington *Titanic*. The Cubist *Titanic*. He was basically a living Museum of the *Titanic*.

He hangs many of these ships on the walls of his lakeside house in Georgia (we live apart). Audrey started going there every summer since she turned five. And every summer, together, they paint, they swim in the lake, they write little limericks. They don't have much else to do since the only toy Audrey's dad ever bought her is some Lego blocks with which they built a giant . . . you guessed it! . . . *Titanic*!

Early this month, while driving in our car, I asked Audrey, "What do you like about going to Georgia?" I like talking to my girl this way, inside our Kia Soul, one-on-one—me asking her questions about random things and her taking her time to answer them without the pressure of context.

I usually get honest answers this way. She tells me, "Well, there're no toys there, you know. And I like it like that. Toys are kind of boring."

To which I said, "Really?"—a part of me all giddy about this new development.

"I build stuff, like out of things I find. You know, like things we usually throw out. It's actually a lot of fun!" She sounded excited. I asked her how she became that way, how she came to not appreciate the conventional toys she used to like so much, like her kitchen sets and her Barbie doll collection.

"I noticed all the tiny windows."

"What windows?"

"On Daddy's *Titanic*. I wanted to build something like that, something that beautiful." **—Jung, Montclair, NJ**

Passing Notes

I was married to a man with a preteen daughter. We had a really difficult time communicating, so I bought a pretty journal and started a letter to her. I left it on her bed and asked her to write back. It opened up a really honest and caring exchange between us. **—Lynda, Charleston, SC**

My mom set up a little wooden box on her dresser through the tween years for my youngest sister, who was quite shy. She could write any questions she had about puberty, for example, on bits of paper and sneak into our parents' room and put her question in the box. My mom would write a response and put it back in the box for my sister to find.

Though it wasn't a strategy my mom needed for me or my other two sisters, it was the perfect solution for my shy sister, who had questions just as we had but didn't want to ask them in person. **—Jess, Burlington, ON, Canada**

When I was a teen, my mother and I had a standing rule. She would not read my diary unless I left it out. This was a win on two fronts. I *never* left it in the common areas where she tidied up. But when I got older and decided it was time to get help for my suicidal and self-harm tendencies but was afraid to start that conversation, all I had to do was leave my journal on her nightstand. The next day, she started the conversation for me. We had a long talk about what I had been dealing with. She had already found a crisis counselor, and together we began the process of finding a long-term therapist. My daughters are now preteens, and we have the same arrangement. **—Megan, Fargo, ND**

I created an email address for each of my kids, and every time I have a great photo, or they do something funny, or they reach a milestone, or I just want to tell them something, I send them an email and put keywords in the subject line. That way, I can always search for keywords—like first word or first tooth or whatever—and pull it up in a flash. And then, of course, I'll eventually give them access to the email as well so that they can read all my messages to them over the years. I often forward them things, too, or bcc them on certain messages.

—Erin, Sacramento, CA

My dad has had a longtime method of getting information through to me that he may have been too nervous to bring up on his own—I think it was his way of saying things to me without me going, "UGH, I KNOW, DAD!"

My room growing up was the attic, and my dad would *always* leave me articles on the stairs. Some examples of articles I vividly remember getting: ones on teenage pregnancy (written by teenagers), one about how hearts stopping during a first experience taking Ecstasy can lead to death, one about how a clean room can equal a happy mind, and some Dear Abby letters. He would sometimes talk to me about what was in the article at a later date and sometimes not.

I'm thirty-two now and my dad still saves me articles for when I visit or when he's coming to see me. These days, the articles are about real estate advice, millennial habits, the struggle of full-time work and parenting, and the benefits of lemon water and a daily walk. I read them all and I always have. Now I try to save him articles, too.

P.S. I should also mention that he would leave me an occasional funny one, or one about a movie or a local community event in between some of the serious content!

—Michelle, Yardley, PA

When I was a child, I rejected my Asian heritage. My mother was quite dismayed and tried a hundred ways to teach me something about our culture. But I refused. Finally, she realized that if I was ever to learn anything about our culture, she was going to have to sneak it in. So she watched me, saw that I loved books, especially fairy tales. Then she went and bought half a dozen Chinese fairy-tale books (translated into English) and put them on the bookshelf in the living room. She knew better than to give them to me—she hoped that I would find them and read them. Well, I did! And when I became an adult, they were one of the few tenuous threads I had to my Asian culture. In fact, they became the threads upon which I built a bridge, because when I became an author, they were the inspiration for my most popular books. So that was definitely a win for my mom!

—**Grace Lin, author of *Where the Mountain Meets the Moon***

We have an Emergency Family Emoji. If one of my teenagers uses it in a text, and they are at a friend's house, it means I need to come get them right away. If they text me a question with the emoji, it means I need to answer no. They need me to be the bad guy sometimes so they don't lose face in front of their friends. It gives them an easy out, and I am not allowed to ask questions. I just get them out of dangerous situations. They know that if they text me that emoji, I will be there, no questions asked. —**Shantell, Salt Lake City, UT**

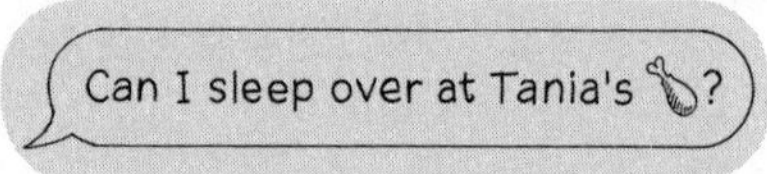

When I was a tween (though we didn't call it that then), I had a very complicated love-hate relationship with slumber parties. I loved the togetherness and the staying up late and the snacks and tricks, but I would often get overwhelmed by a certain point, feel tired and lonely, and really want to go home. But who can admit they want to go home? Total loser move.

My mom came up with an ingenious plan and saved me from many a late-night meltdown. The deal was: When I arrived for the party, I'd say I wasn't sure I could stay overnight, I had to check in with my mom later. And then if I wanted to go home, I'd call my mom and say, "Do I have to come home or can I stay?" and she would say, "I want you to come home; I'm going to come and pick you up now."

If I was having a good time, I just never made the call and I looked like kind of a badass. If I was miserable, I made my mom look totally mean, and no one needed to know that I was a bit of a baby. —Jacqueline, Toronto, ON, Canada

Don't Ask, Do Tell

In fourth grade, my son started at a new school, after aging out of an amazing public Montessori school that he had attended for six years. The new school was a bad fit for him, but he didn't really share a lot of what was going on with us. Instead he was just always sad or angry, and we mostly didn't know why. We tried, unsuccessfully, to work with the school—and then later tried, unsuccessfully, to get him into a different school. At the beginning of February, we pulled him out of school to temporarily homeschool because he was so anxious all the time. (We did this even though we both work, if that helps to give you a sense of our desperation.)

We made a deal that if he got all his work done by Thursday, he could have Fridays off. Many Friday mornings, he and I would each take a book to a coffee shop and hang out over coffee while his sister was in school. And he would talk. This is how I began to learn what had upset him.

Now regular one-on-one coffee dates are our thing. We also play cards and go for walks. If I ask questions, though, I ruin everything. **—Katie, South Bend, IN**

My mother was and is one of the coolest chicks I know, and when I was a teenager, she was pretty easygoing. But she had two rules: no smoking cigarettes and no tattoos. So, of course, on my eighteenth birthday, I had to get that little tribal tattoo on the inside of my right ankle. I spent two years hiding it with ankle bracelets and socks, keeping my body in a position where the inside of my right ankle wasn't in her eyesight and sweating while trying on shoes at the mall with her.

One day I decided that enough was enough and I had to tell her. We were at a family friend's pool party, and while we were changing into our suits, I said, "Mom, I have to tell you something."

I saw the blood drain from her face, and she shakily said, "What?"

I said, "I have a tattoo."

And she said, "I know! Your sister told me the day after you got it! I thought you were going to tell me you were pregnant! So let's see it."

And then she proceeded to tell me that the punishment for it was watching me squirm for the past two years!

—Tabitha, Delray Beach, FL

I was a teenager in the '90s and a devoted fan of *Beverly Hills 90210*. I can only imagine it was not on the top of my mom's list of must-watch shows. But every week, without fail, she would watch with me and talk about the different things being done by—and happening to—Brenda and Brandon and friends.

Looking back, I see how this was such a natural way for her to bring up a wide variety of topics that might have been much more awkward to discuss under different circumstances. And it didn't hurt that she would usually rub my feet while we watched. It definitely ensured I was always happy to have her watch "9-0" with me! **—Stephanie, Morton Grove, IL**

My mom and I were very close, even when I was a teenager, and two things really helped with that. We watched *Oprah* together after school most days while I did homework. During commercial breaks, and sometimes even during part of the news show that followed, we would get into discussions based on the show topic. When the show ended, it was the end of an era for us. I also loved going grocery shopping with her. It was quality time together where we talked, but I also got the great grocery-shopping and meal-planning skills that I now use with my own family! **—Sarah, Maryland**

My mom used this trick in middle school and high school to get me to tell her about virtually every dishonorable or mischievous thing I'd done lately. She would simply ask me, "Is there anything you want to tell me?" I would usually respond, "Well, what do you know?" And then she'd tell me things would go easier for me if she heard it directly from me. Since I didn't know what she did or did not know, I'd just tell her everything to get ahead of the story and put my own spin on it. She later told me that she rarely knew anything. *Damn!*

—Hannah, Fairbanks, AK

I have a seventeen-year-old foster daughter who lives in a group home. She gets in trouble a lot more than other kids because she has the entire state welfare system watching everything she does, and a lot of times she feels terrible about letting down all of the adults around her. Every time she does something "wrong," I try to recount a story of something bad I did as a teen. Honestly, I try to one-up her. I think it's working? LOL. Now, after about a year of this, she comes to me first to tell me about any incidents and then follows up with "What would you have done?" questions, which is an amazing invite from a teen and allows us space to talk openly about our fuckups, regrets, and how we can become better people.

—Jane, Los Angeles, CA

My sister told my mom *everything* growing up. I did not. My mom had to find other ways to get the information about my life. She happened to be the mom who drove my friends and me everywhere. She has since told me that this is where she found out the gossip. Apparently, no matter how quiet we thought we were being, she heard it. She would then later conveniently tell me a story that would help me with the life problems I was having, dissuade me from doing whatever stupid idea I had planned, or show me she was once a teenager just like me. She must have been pretty good, because I never found out until she told me all about it when I became pregnant.

—Marisa, Nashville, TN

Chapter 10

The Art of Getting It On as a Parent

Do we really need to explain this one?

REMEMBER THAT EPISIOTOMY I told you about in the introduction to this book? How they had to recut and restitch me a week after I gave birth because the original stitches had busted open? It took two months for that wound to heal. But long after I could sit flat on my bottom and run up a flight of stairs, something else was a problem: sex.

My midwife had warned me to expect sex to be painful for up to a year. But the more I did it, she told me, the more my scar tissue would stretch and the better it would feel. *Okay,* I thought. *I'll just fake it till I make it.* But, as it turns out, faking it is pretty impossible when you feel like . . . well, like you're being stabbed in the vagina.

Let me pause for a second and say that I know many women suffer from sexual dysfunction—that they can't have penetrative intercourse without pain. For me, this was new. I became terrified of intimacy. I used breastfeeding and sleep deprivation as an excuse. "Sorry, honey, boobs are leaking and I'm pooped." But the truth is, I couldn't imagine ever having sex again. I couldn't even bear to think about *other* people having sex. If my husband and I were watching a movie, I'd avert my eyes during make-out scenes. Even watching passionate kissing would remind me of the unbearably sharp pain I sometimes felt between my legs. Actually, any form of romantic touch could send me over the edge. I remember going to the theater with my husband, and the guy in front of us was tenderly stroking his date's neck. It was as irritating to me as if someone had been kicking the back of my chair. *Could you stop it already? I'm trying to watch a show here!*

I saw doctor after doctor, asking what was wrong, what could be done. The first one kept me waiting pantsless on a table for an hour and was irritated to find that when she finally came to examine me, I was nursing the baby.

"I can come back later, when you're done," she quipped.

"No, I'm ready," I said. I lay back, knees spread, my daughter still suctioned to my chest.

The doctor took a quick look, poked around, and said nonchalantly, "The scar tissue's too tight. We'll just give you another little snip." She air-scissored her fingers.

"Another little snip"? The last thing I wanted was more cutting. Plus, snipping would only add more scar tissue—and I was skeptical that adding more scar tissue would actually help my situation.

The next doctor told me I looked absolutely normal. There was no reason I should be in pain. But since I *was* in pain, the thing I should do was have another baby. As soon as possible. Because then I'd tear open along my scar line. And tears, apparently, heal better than incisions.

"But I don't think I *want* another baby," I told her.

"Wow," she said, as if she'd never met a mom who didn't crave multiple children. "This really did a number on you, huh?"

Another doctor told me I was in pain because I was a redhead and I had sensitive skin. She prescribed me estrogen cream, which was supposed to soften the scar tissue. If that didn't work, we'd move on to testosterone cream. Though that could really overboost my sex drive, she told me—and possibly cause facial hair growth. If the hormone creams didn't work, she suggested a little surgery. We'd simply graft some skin from the inside of my vagina and pull it over the scar to the outside to create a little extra padding over the injury.

"You'll never be a centerfold model," she said chuckling, "but it should work."

Of course, there was always the very big chance that it would do the opposite of work. Because: even *more* scar tissue.

None of these doctors' options felt like real options. Though I will admit, I spent hours fantasizing over the idea that having another baby could save me—if only we could guarantee that the baby would definitely tear open my episiotomy. Which, when you think about it, wishing to be vaginally torn apart is pretty messed up.

My next wish was that sex was not a thing. And I don't mean I just wished that I didn't have to do it anymore; I wished it was a thing that humans would stop doing, period. Because then maybe I wouldn't feel so much pressure to perform.

But I kept trying to perform. Sometimes I'd shut my eyes, grit my teeth, and hold my breath through the pain. Of course, my husband could tell that's what I was doing, and being the good guy that he is, he said he didn't want to do it if he was hurting me.

I felt bad, though, that my pain meant he was denied pleasure. This wasn't what he'd signed up for when we got married. What if he started looking for sex elsewhere? He said he wouldn't, that he wanted us to figure this out together—but what if we never figured it out?

"I don't want you to do anything you don't want to do," he'd say.

And so . . . I didn't. For a full year.

All in all, it was three years of ouchy sex or no sex at all. During that time, I did not feel like myself. Or, I was another version of myself. Ghostlier. Number. Deader. It was as if all the parts of me that were light and fun and flirty had evaporated, and all that remained were the caregiving parts—providing food, cleaning up poop, and teaching a tiny person not to be a jerk.

One day, I was looking on a local Listserv and I saw someone mention a gynecologist she liked. How attentive she was, what a good listener. That didn't describe any gyno I'd ever seen, so I made an appointment. This doctor, a freckly woman about my age, was the gyno of my dreams. She did listen—to every detail of my sob story. Without rushing me. She shook her head in dismay at every horrible solution I'd heard from other doctors. She agreed with the theory that having another baby could help, but she also thought that wasn't the best reason to create a human. And this was all before she even had me get undressed.

"You're really mangled down there," she said when she examined me. "You're actually . . . not anatomical." She must've seen my face drop because she quickly added, "I know that's not a thing you want to hear about your vagina. But the way you were put back together is . . . off."

"Off," while certainly better than "mangled," is also not a thing you want to hear about your vagina.

This doctor suggested that I try pelvic floor physical therapy. She also gave me the number of her mentor, a vulvar surgeon. But the physical therapist and the surgeon only agreed on this: that I really should just see one and not the other. The therapist believed I could be treated without medical procedures; the doctor thought physical therapy was a bunch of baloney. As it turned out, I needed them both.

I had never heard of pelvic floor physical therapy. I wish I'd found out about it sooner. In fact, I wish it was an option for all postpartum women. Many postpartum injuries can be healed with the alignment and muscle manipulation you get from physical therapy. And, man, it helped me a ton. But some injuries need an extra push.

Enter the vulvar surgeon—a red-faced man with receding white hair and pointy eyebrows like the Count from *Sesame Street*. As soon as he got his pudgy gloved fingers inside me, he seemed to know what the problem was.

"A neuroma," he told me with a toothy grin.

The Count squeezed one spot between his fingertips. The tenderest spot. "That hurt?" he asked.

"Yes!" I shouted, arching my back.

"Right . . . there?" He squeezed harder.

"Yes, yes! There!"

He let go. "Yep, that's a neuroma."

A neuroma is a thing that can happen in scar tissue, where your nerves get kinda balled up and form a painful lump under your skin. It's one of the most basic injuries you can get from surgery of any kind, anywhere on your body. It is astonishing that it took three years for someone to catch something this common.

"You're lucky you found me," the Count said back in his office, with the distinct cockiness of a guy who fixes vaginas for a living. "Most women just give up on sex forever. Good for you for being persistent."

I asked him what he thought about the have-another-baby theory, adding that I didn't know yet if I wanted one.

"Of course you don't!" he said. "How could you possibly know if you want another baby if you can't even do the thing that would get you one?" Exactly!

The Count asked me for the names and addresses of the doctors who'd misdiagnosed me, which he later used to write them letters, basically telling them that they were dumbasses—a thing I had no idea doctors did to each other. I imagined Dr. We'll-Just-Snip-You, Dr. This-Really-Did-a-Number-on-You, Dr. You'll-Never-Be-a-Centerfold, and Dr. I-Made-You-Unanatomical-in-the-First-Place sitting at their desks in cushy chairs, reading the letter with their heads in their hands, wondering how they could've been so stupid as to miss a neuroma. A neuroma!

The Count scheduled me for a procedure. He said he'd rub two kinds of medicine into the neuroma—cortisone and Marcaine—and, bam, that should take care of my pain.

A few weeks later, I went to the hospital and let this guy put me under and do his thing.

When I woke up, he told me that he'd "mashed that medicine in there pretty good," so it might hurt once the anesthesia wore off.

The pain was excruciating—I spent a week lying in bed with an ice pack between my legs. At my checkup with the Count I lay on his exam table, asking him why it wasn't better yet.

"Ooh," he said, turning his head in what I can only describe as delighted disgust. "Looks like someone hit you with a baseball bat!" The someone who made me look like that, of course, was *him*. He assured me the bruises would heal soon and told me to get dressed and meet him at the front desk with my husband, who'd driven me to the appointment. There, the Count presented us with six sample packets of lube. Three kinds, two of each. "Use these," he said. "You'll need 'em."

The Count turned to my husband. "No penetration," he said sternly. "Not yet. Wait at least a couple of weeks. Even if she thinks she's ready. I mean it."

"Okay," my husband said, with a nervous laugh.

But the Count wasn't done. "Just the tip at first. That's all. You stop. Then you ease back in a little at a time."

"Got it," my husband said.

We turned to leave. But we only went a few steps before the Count shouted, "Oh, wait!" He caught up with us, pulling one of the packets from my hand. "Careful with this one. It's sticky. Seriously, I've spent like an hour in the shower trying to rinse this stuff off." He mimed a scrubbing motion over his crotch. Not a thing I wanted to picture the Count doing . . . but point taken. "Go make lots of babies!" he called to us as we finally walked out the door.

Dude had a weird bedside manner. But. That no-penetration thing worked. For a while, sex was still scary as shit. But the gradual ramping-it-up technique made it less so. Until, eventually, things felt normal—mangled vagina or not.

The truth is, though, I'd had a breakthrough of my own just months before the Count worked his magic. A win that came in the unlikely form of Hurricane Sandy, the "superstorm" that ravaged the Northeast a couple of days before Halloween in 2012.

That night, my husband and I pulled Sasha's mattress out of her crib and moved it to the floor in our bedroom—we were afraid of a tree branch or something crashing through her window. And then there we were: child sleeping, no power, no heat.

We went to the living room, made a fire. Laid some blankets on the rug. Took off our clothes, cozied up. Outside, transformers were exploding. Hundred-year-old trees were ripping out of sidewalks, crashing into roofs. Inside, I was taking a giant risk. I was reacquainting my body with my husband's, something I hadn't had the guts to do in years. I remember sort of talking myself into it—not in a get-this-over-with way, but in a give-this-a-chance way. Because no matter how much I wished it, the world isn't gonna stop having sex. And . . . if I don't get flattened by a gigantic tree trunk tonight, it might just be worth getting another doctor's opinion. Yes, it'll suck if I find out there's no real solution to this problem. But what if there is? What a shame it would be to live the rest of my life not having found it. To just give in forever to the food-feeding, poop-cleaning, manners-teaching version of myself.

As it turned out, I didn't have to.

Sneaking Around

My husband and I are the parents of twins. Pre-kids, we had a very active and healthy sex life. Post-twins, we were too tired to have sex. We used to have morning sex, but now we're too afraid of waking them. Their bedroom is across the hall from ours.

These days, since I work from home, we meet up for a quickie when my husband has an afternoon break from work. We call it "afternoon delight" as our sly way of talking about our rendezvous. Pre-kids, we used to take whole days off and just have sex. Now that our girls are in daycare full-time, we pick a day to play hooky from work and sleep in, have sex, eat lunch out, then have sex again. It's something we really look forward to, and seeing a midday movie together is better than a date-night movie because it's usually just us at the movie theater! **—Jennifer, Burbank, CA**

We have a baby and a seven-year-old. I do not remember the last time we had bedtime sex; we're just too tired. We do it during the middle of the day on the weekends, when the time is just right . . . *"niño afuera, niña durmiendo"* (big kid outside, little kid sleeping). So grateful for the neighbors who don't mind our kid hanging out with their kids in their yards. If they only knew. **—Anonymous, USA**

My husband and I both work full-time jobs as professors and have two little kids. Sometimes it can be very hard to find time together, and going out on dates, while nice, can be exhausting and expensive. So we have begun to use some of the time the kids are in daycare to have "microdates." Our daycare doesn't close until 6:00 p.m., so days when we can get out of work early—by 4:45 or 5:00 p.m.—we will meet up at a restaurant or bar near the daycare, have one drink, and share an appetizer. Having these times to reconnect has been amazing, especially during the academic year. While these microdates do not lead to immediate trysts (need to pick up the kids!), they certainly do help us stay connected and often lead to some playtime later in the evenings after the kids have gone to bed.

—Christine, Lancaster, PA

My husband came home from work the other day ready to get it on. My daughter is eighteen months old and deaf. So I dropped her in the crib with twenty books, grabbed the monitor, and said, "See you soon." Some may say that is neglectful; I say it's resourceful. Happy parents make happy children.

—**Seila, Washington**

As kids get older, they don't need eyes on them 24-7. Now's the time to steal moments of intimacy. Maybe you both have to go to the garage for something—take a moment to touch and kiss passionately. Maybe you are facing away from the kid(s) and your partner isn't. Give them a look or a touch that only you two can see or feel. It can be just a second or two; be creative. Do this repeatedly throughout the day. It can feel a bit forbidden and secretive. By the end of the day, you may have a stronger desire for something other than sleep.

—**Satisfied Mom, San Diego, CA**

My husband and I did *not* co-sleep, but when we had our child in a bassinet in our room, I was getting frustrated with the lack of sex in our lives. I remember waking my husband up, having made a pallet in the nursery—a room that was not being used. We turned on the monitor and just moved the event from our bedroom to the baby's!

—**Lynette, Lexington, KY**

My husband and I are unwilling participants in a co-sleeping situation with our four-year-old daughter. She was never a good sleeper but wasn't as intrusive until she escaped the confines of her crib at three years old. Several months ago, monsters began invading her room, and now, after battling her nightly for weeks, she is a permanent fixture in our bed.

This new sleeping arrangement has forced us to revert back to fooling around like when we lived with our parents. Our closet is inside our master bedroom. We sneak in after she is sleeping, then close the closet door. (This is a walk-in closet, so we aren't among the hangers—but this situation is not particularly romantic or sexy, not to mention the rug burn.)

Our guest bedroom sees some action as well but isn't the first choice because the door has a terribly loud squeak that has not been fixed because neither of us thinks about it until we are trying to close it ever so quietly. We had relatives visiting us recently and decided to have an overdue date night. On the way to the restaurant, we stopped to put gas in the car and ended up messing around in the gas station car wash.

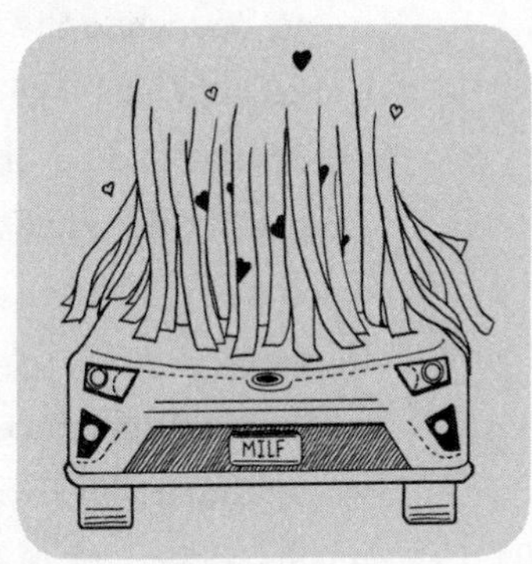

Our sex life is basically taking advantage of any second of alone time. It isn't ideal, but we have bonded in a weird way to overcome the "cock-blocker" (I can't believe I just typed that) in our bed.

—Anonymous, North Carolina

We bought a sleeper sofa so we can have sex comfortably in the living room while our seven-month-old sleeps in our bed. We keep a blanket to cover the couch so we don't make a mess. **—Katie, Berkeley, CA**

We chose to co-sleep with our daughter mostly by accident. I had a long labor that ended in a C-section after a failed epidural. Which mostly meant that once I made it into bed, I was not moving. So for nighttime feedings, my husband had to get the baby and bring her to me. But then he fell back to sleep and so she just stayed in our bed.

As for sex, while we were bed-sharing with the children, it was on some level easier than it's been with the kids at their current ages of six and nine. (They have never met a closed door that they don't want to open.) It boiled down to not having sex in our bed; we had sex on the couch. Or we had sex in the shower. Or we'd sneak away to have a quickie in our bed while the kids were playing in the living room. It worked out just fine because we never really liked having sex in the middle of the night after getting ready for bed. And while the kids were young, my husband was a school teacher while I went to school. We didn't have time for morning sex.

So my experience was that sex while co-sleeping really wasn't that tricky. Figuring out a way to share the blankets was much harder. **—Anonymous, Seattle, WA**

We have co-slept with all three of our kids to some extent. I think the fact that co-sleeping forces you to find a place to "do it" outside the bedroom helps keep things spicy. In fact, when one of our kids insisted on sleeping in the living room for several months, we had to go up to her room. Not sure if that was particularly sexy, but you gotta do what you gotta do! I think the sneaking around makes you feel a little bit like a teenager again and does add to the excitement. And regular sex is so key to keeping yourself sane and feeling like an adult while living with small humans. For whatever reason, I think we are having better sex now (after ten years of marriage and three kids) than we ever have before. **—Anna, Kentucky**

We hire a babysitter for four to six hours and book a hotel room for the night. Even though we don't sleep overnight in the hotel room, it provides some much-needed child-free connection time. We can be as loud as we want, eat room service or takeout, and enjoy some adult time together. It's expensive but worth it once in a while to rekindle our romance. Especially since we have three kids, one of which is a baby co-sleeping with us right now. **—Anonymous, Sacramento, CA**

Our three-year-old ninja (read: kicks, hits, and yells in her sleep) is still part-time co-sleeping. She comes into our bed each night around 2:00 or 3:00 a.m. because she's had a nightmare or wants comfort. Every time we were awake enough to carry her back to her own bed, she would inevitability wake up and run back to our room a short time later. Just before the arrival of our second baby, we were desperate for a solution. Our reward magnet board didn't seem to matter much to her; our prize incentive system didn't seem to motivate her. She can hurl herself over the baby gate that's installed on her bedroom door, and I don't have the heart to lock her in her room just to hear her scream for us at 3:00 a.m.

Our solution was to get out her old crib mattress and put it on the floor next to our bed and call it her "camping mat." We sold it to her as this cool new place to sleep while still being close to Mom and Dad. Now when she comes for her 3:00 a.m.

snuggles, she's in our bed for a short time and then we move her down to her camping mat.

So sex for us is "scheduled" early in the night (shortly after bedtime), while both kids are in their deepest sleep and least likely to wake up or need to come to our bed for any reason.

—Sara, Danville, CA

My husband, Jeff, and I are the parents of two children. Both of them were co-sleepers when they were little. With my son, the oldest, we kept a large plush footstool at the edge of the bed. Whenever he would fall asleep and we were feeling frisky, we would roll him onto it and roll it into his bedroom. Things were a bit harder when his sister was born. We still managed to wheel him to his room, but his sister was a lighter sleeper and didn't transport as easily. We would either sneak out of the room to other rooms of the house or depend on date nights for our sexual escapades. Now that they are older—twelve and ten—it's much easier. They sleep in their own bedrooms.

—Michelle, Noble, IL

Parenthood Is Erotic . . . Really!

My hubby sends me meeting notices for sex on our family Google calendar. They look like this:

Example 1:

Invitation: Hanky-panky

When: Tue Jun 6, 2017 9:30–10pm

WHERE: Downstairs shower [Google offers an unhelpful map option link here]

NOTES: Astroglide already confirmed he will be in attendance.

Example 2:

INVITATION: Back rub and blindfold hanky-panky

WHEN: Wed Oct 4, 2017 9:30–10:30pm

WHERE: You will be located on your back, on top, on bottom, and possibly a number of other places

They make me laugh every time. And since they are in the calendar, we are motivated to follow through with them.

—LIBBIE, SAINT PAUL, MN

We are a co-sleeping family, and this was something that we wanted to do even before our daughter was born. For the first three years of being parents, we lived in a small two-bedroom apartment. All of us slept in the main bedroom, but the second room was for miscellaneous things like boxes that we'd never unpacked, the diaper-changing area, laundry that hadn't been folded, and a futon. The futon was there mainly for when the grandparents came to visit us (they live in Toronto, about a four-and-a-half-hour drive away). But usually no one sleeps on the futon, and that's where we'd have sex after we put our daughter to bed. It's also an incentive to fold the laundry—like, "If we can clear off the clean clothes from the futon, we get to have sex."

—JOYCE, OTTAWA, ON, CANADA

My husband and I are co-sleepers with a two-year-old and have another on the way. We've had to get *very* creative to keep our sex life active. The first thing I did was explain to my husband that he has to get me out of "mom" mode and into "wife/sexy" mode. So foreplay really helps keep us active! We start dropping signals whenever we're feeling frisky. Maybe a gentle butt smack or a light hair tug. Our weirdest hint that we're "ready to go" is to ask each other if we want to play *Mario Kart*! We're very competitive and somewhat equally matched at gaming, so it's not too difficult to switch from the excitement of games on the couch to games in the bed! My husband and I have been together for ten years, since college, so these types of competitive foreplay games have been going on for a long time, but now we're able to use them without being obvious to anyone but ourselves (we hope!). **—Kelsie, Japan**

Do You Agree to These Sexy-ish Terms?

After the birth of my second kid, I started running as a means to get exercise and me time. That put pressure on an already full schedule, but my husband and I made a deal. Every evening that he helped with the kids so that I could go for a run, he was granted automatic sex with no excuses from me. It was a great motivator for us both! **—Allison, Raleigh, NC**

Shortly after becoming pregnant with our third child, my first husband and I knew that though we weren't suited as husband and wife, we were well suited as friends and co-parents. We had a lovely separation ceremony, filed the papers for divorce, and I soon remarried. We had a beautiful wedding, and then we all continued to live together and raise the kids for the next seven years. (Pretty big house with a guest house.) We happily shared meals and parenting duties. It was definitely a parenting win, for us and for the kids, and you've got to admit, a little weird. **—Wendy, Arizona**

The secret to a healthy sex life is sleeping in twin beds, side by side, like Rob and Laura in *The Dick Van Dyke Show* (which my toddler calls *The Bing Dite Dite Show*). They're beautiful beds. Distressed white headboards with big European square pillows. We call it our French-countryside bedroom because it's so romantic.

It was accidental at first. I was co-sleeping with a breastfeeding baby, and there wasn't room for my husband in our double bed. So we got an extra twin mattress. Then, once my son was sleeping on his own but still waking up during the night to be comforted, I retreated to the twin mattress and let my husband take over. At least one person slept well at all times, which made sex doable. Eventually, everyone was sleeping through the night, just in separate, haphazard locations, and the sex was great. After our son went to bed, my husband and I were doing it on the living room floor in front of the fireplace, with a little sofa foreplay beforehand—all possible because we were getting enough rest. So when it came time to either upgrade to a queen or two twins, we chose the latter, and we love it. My husband can get up in the middle of the night for a million bathroom trips, and I never wake up. I can sleep on a medium mattress, he on a soft. I can fall asleep to a silenced Netflix show with subtitles without keeping him up. I'm telling you, I don't know why we didn't do this earlier. **—Jasara, Pensacola, FL**

I'm an early-bird nurse; my man is a night-owl programmer. He's still asleep when I leave for work, I'm knocked out before he's off work, and our preschoolers are awake the rest of the time. I read that before electric lights, people used to go to bed with the sun, awaken for a few hours, and then have a second sleep, and that lovemaking was common during that nighttime wakening. So every now and then, I give him the little elbow-elbow, wink-wink, "Wake me up when you come to bed," and we have a little midnight meetup. (This is lovely because I, the sleepier person, have given the okay beforehand.)

—Anonymous, Texas

I have a long history of co-sleeping while trying to maintain a sex life, and it's kind of . . . bumpy. My oldest child is thirteen, and his dad and I were just not ready to be together when I got pregnant at twenty-two. I had sole control over the sleep situation for the first years of parenthood as a single mom. I had never planned to co-sleep, but I was struggling to breastfeed, and I would often pull him into bed with me. I soon found that I was really comfortable with it.

When he was two, I bought him a race car bed and would lie down with him in it every night and snuggle him to sleep. Sometimes I'd fall asleep, too, which was murder on my neck and back or my legs that had been dangling off at some weird angle. Many nights I'd wake up to my phone buzzing to meet up with someone I was seeing for some drinks and, likely, sex. Fun times trying to put myself together after falling asleep on a race car bed, explaining the pillowcase crease marks on my cheek. My mom lived with me, so I'd leave her a note and head out around 11:00 p.m. or so, and was always home before

4:00 a.m., which was my son's usual first wake time, when he'd come climb into bed with me. Did I mention I had a twin bed in his room?

When my son was four, his dad and I married, and I had to confess that we were still room-sharing. My spouse insisted it was time for our son to sleep in his own room. That transition was tough for both my son and me. Soon I was pregnant with our second child, and then our third, and the co-sleeping frightened my husband, so I did it less, and always had to put the babes in their beds if I wanted sex. My husband is super private about sex, but I'm a doula—I tend to be pretty open. I wasn't all that concerned about having a baby in the room, but he was of the mind-set that it would screw our kids up to know that their parents are sexual.

One night, my husband brought our two-year-old daughter into our bed. She had a fever, and he wanted to keep her close. (This had always been my approach, but it was the first time he'd done it.) Shortly thereafter, we had our fourth baby, and I found we had segued into full-time co-sleeping. Suddenly my spouse was a pro at arranging pillows, blankets, and baby so that we could roll around a little and just be naked together. He knew he had to place himself between me and the baby or risk fluttering eyes catching sight of my nipple, and then it would all be over. And honestly, we did stop like every three seconds to check on him. Then we did the thing where you remove one side of the crib and attach it to the bed, making the crib mattress level with the bed (so it's a crib-size co-sleeper). It was a perfect setup. We had become great at all kinds of sex without shaking the bed, and all it took was for me to roll the baby into the crib and maybe strategically angle a pillow.

We have no problem changing up the location or staying up late together after getting everyone to sleep. We run into the bathroom and enjoy the use of the mirror. We've had sex in the car in parking garages on date nights, in the backyard under the stars, in his "workshop" (aka the garage), in the kitchen against the wall while cookies are baking in the oven.

Now our fifth baby is fifteen months old, and I was ready for her to start sleeping on her own when she turned one—and it worked! We're still masters of the silent romp, but with baby number five, it was a full year before I was into sex. My nipples were off-limits, I really wasn't that into vaginal penetration, and my orgasms were mild and hardly worth the effort. So we developed a rotation of activities I could tolerate—rear entry and anal (because of the wonderful back rubs I would get during that), fellatio, and *boob sex*. I don't even know if there's a real name for it, but I learned that I love boob sex. So weird, right? But when I have zero libido and he has *all the libido*, and neither of us has much energy, boob sex is what we do, and it's fun.

Nights when there are kids in the middle and we're on the outside are an acknowledgment that there will be no sex that night, but the hand-holding over their sleeping bodies is amazing. **—Stephanie, Texas**

Chapter 11

The Art of Helping Your Kid Not Be a Kid

Giving your baby the space to grow up, while setting boundaries that (hopefully) won't backfire

THERE IS A FAMILY I've heard of. I don't know their last name or how to track them down. Someone once told me about a tradition of theirs—but since I can't get them to tell me about it directly, I'm gonna go off of what I was told by a friend of a friend and share it with you as I imagine it went down.

Let's call this family the Smiths. The Smiths were respectful folks. They didn't curse—or they tried their darndest to keep it in check. But sometimes Donny Smith would do something so inconsiderate, Daddy Smith would be tempted to explode with a "What the fuck did you do *that* for?!" Instead, Dad would grit his teeth and say, "Donny, I need you to think about your actions and how they affect other people in this family."

Donny's sister, Sonia Smith, would hear this from her room and think, "Shit, why does *he* always get off so easy? That's fucked up!" She'd shout downstairs, "No fair! You're so much harder on me, just 'cause I'm a girl."

And Mama Smith . . . well, she'd be in the kitchen trying to tune it all out, but she'd be thinking, "Dammit all to fucking hell!"

After big moments of tension, the Smiths would apologize to each other and mend the ruptures. But their favorite, most healing time as a family—the time they felt closest—came once a year, on New Year's Day, when they baked a cake. A "fuck" cake.

They rotated who got to pick the flavor of the cake, but the flavor didn't matter, really. It was all about the icing. Mama Smith had bought a fancy pastry-decorating set, with frosting bags and different shaped tips. She never used them to ice cupcakes or cookies; they were exclusively for the fuck cake. Every January 1, the batter went into a pan, the pan into the oven, and the Smiths watched whatever television series happened to be on marathon, as they eagerly waited for the cake to cook and cool. By mid-afternoon, it was ready, and they'd all stand around it, icing bags in hand, and they'd write all the words they'd been dying to say aloud but had (mostly) kept to themselves.

No words were off-limits, but it was understood that on this cake, words were just words; they were not directed at anyone.

Every once in a while, Mama would see something one of her kids had written and she'd go, "Oh, good one!" And she'd add it in her teacherly print. (Yes, she taught third grade.) She'd laugh to herself, imagining what her students would think if they could see her writing these things!

After the cake was completely covered in foul-mouthed graffiti, the Smiths each had a giant slice, plus extra helpings. The vulgar dessert rarely lasted more than a day—but if anything *was* left, the Smiths would finish it off at breakfast the next morning.

Ever since I heard about the fuck cake, I've been tempted to adopt it as a family tradition of my own. Though in our house, cursing is not a once-a-year occurrence. Nor do I want it to be.

Growing up with my parents, cursing was just a part of everyday language. In fact, legend has it, my first word was "shit." I was born in Brooklyn, and apparently when we were in the car and my dad was hunting for a parking spot near our apartment one night, I started chirping from my car seat: "Shit. Shit. Shit . . ." My dad, who realized it might be better for me to be potty-trained before I developed a potty mouth, decided he'd better start curbing his road rage. Which, I'm told, he did—briefly. But I remember my parents cursing a lot when I was a kid—yes, about traffic, but also about the news, about work, about random jerks at the grocery store. Somehow, though, I figured out that those words were grown-up words.

When I became a parent, I needed to decide how I felt about cursing in front of my child. And I decided I mostly felt fine about it. I see cursing as a part of learning vocabulary. These words have meaning and power. And if you overuse them (which maybe I do sometimes), they lose their power (which is maybe a good thing, too). What I hadn't thought about is how I would react if I heard my daughter cursing.

Recently, Sasha's been all about Lorde's album *Melodrama*. Now, I know I could've played her the clean version. But I didn't. And so last summer, on a road trip, we were blasting Lorde, when Sasha started singing "blowin' shit up with homemade d-d-d-dynamite." My husband and I shot each other looks.

"We okay with that?" he asked.

"I think so?" I said.

"Sasha, you can sing it like that when you're with us," he told her, "but not with your friends, okay?"

When she's with friends, she's supposed to leave the curse words out or replace "shit" with "stuff." We'll see how that goes. I'm not too worried: She often mishears lyrics and makes them clean all on her own without realizing it.

Then there was the time I taught her the word "bitch." On purpose. All in the interest of a punch line.

Sasha had just started second grade and she loved her new teacher. She asked me if I ever had a teacher I didn't like, because she couldn't imagine that (lucky kid). I said, "Yeah, my worst teacher was in second grade, when I was your age." I told Sasha the teacher was really strict—is that a word kids use for teachers anymore?—and that her name was Mrs. Middleditch. But we used to call her something else that rhymed.

"What did you call her?" Sasha asked.

That's when I found myself saying, "Have you ever heard the word 'bitch'?"

The truth is, I really enjoyed letting her in on this word myself rather than waiting for her to hear it for the first time from another kid, possibly aimed at her—which is how I first heard it.

The way I see it, we're giving Sasha access to "grown-up" language a little bit at a time. Just like she'll learn about sex a little bit at a time, and death a little bit at a time, and disappointment and responsibility a little bit at a time. Maybe we'll work a fuck cake into the mix at some point, if we feel the need to give her a special outlet for certain words. But I very much look forward to the day when we're sitting at the kitchen counter drinking coffee and reading magazines, and she looks up from her article and goes, "Whoa, that's fucked up," and it seems completely normal.

You're Pubescent; Let's Party!

I threw period parties for my three daughters. When each girl experienced her first period, we had a family party. A black forest cake, a gift box of pads—and Urge Overkill's "Girl, You'll Be a Woman Soon" blasting on the stereo. The lighthearted parties marked the honored daughter's menses and maturity and were our family's way to ensure the milestone moments would be remembered with smiles, not shame and secrecy. The celebration helped make the monthly mayhem going forward a wee bit less dreadful, too—for all of us. To this day, my three daughters—all in their thirties now—fondly recall their offbeat initiation into womanhood.

—**Lisa, Colorado Springs, CO**

It's a tradition in my family that when a girl gets her first period, she has a tea party thrown in her honor. All adult female friends and relatives get dressed up, come over, and enjoy tea and little cakes, cookies, and sandwiches. Usually, girls who haven't gotten their periods aren't included, so the party feels like a special initiation into the world of womanhood. One's own tea party can feel somewhat embarrassing, but a cousin's tea party, for example, is a blast! —**Kristin, Waterbury, VT**

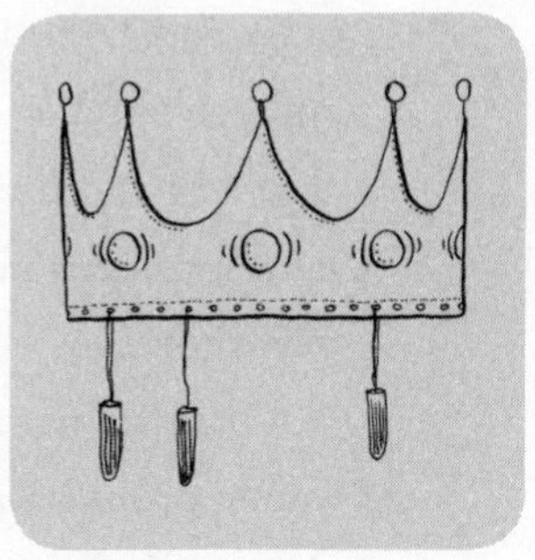

My son is seventeen years old, and recently, many lubricating substances have gone missing in our house. Today I walked into his room to get his laundry and found *my* jar of virgin coconut oil on his bookshelf (without a spoon, I might add . . .). I am not a prude, nor do I care how often my teenage son is in need of these items, but I *am* tired of him pilfering my stuff. So I went to the store and made him a gift basket—lube, lotion, hand repair cream (just in case), coconut-scented hand sanitizer, socks (more absorbent than tissues), baby wipes, and the most recent issue of *Cosmo*. I put it all in a basket with a card that read "Now you don't have to steal my coconut oil!! XOXO, Mom."

When he found it, he came walking through the kitchen, smiling and blushing with the remaining coconut oil and said, "I'm just going to throw this away." When he came back inside, he said, "You're evil, but really funny."

Every so often I get it right. **—Caroline, Richmond, VA**

I have always been very open and honest with my now newly pubescent thirteen-year-old son about sex and genitalia. I have approached the discussion of puberty and sex with nonchalance and frankness. And I certainly never wanted him to feel any shame about his body or having sexual feelings once puberty set in.

One day, as my older son was hanging out on the couch, watching his baby brother run around naked between diaper changes, he told me, "Charlie's penis is so small!"

"Well, yes," I said. "His penis is small because he's so little. The penis does enlarge somewhat during puberty. So by comparison, it must seem really small."

"And it certainly doesn't help that I'm walking around with an erection most of the time!"

We chuckled about his pubescent "predicament," but inwardly I was shocked he would reveal that to me, his mom. I don't often feel like I got something right when it comes to parenting, but in that moment I felt pretty downright proud of myself. I expected him to shut down as his body began to change, but he was continuing to let me in. **—Lulu, Maplewood, NJ**

I remember asking my parents if I could start shaving my legs. I was in the fourth or fifth grade, so it was probably a bit early to need this sort of grooming, but I had seen that many of my brother's friends had shaved legs and I was ready to be a teenager. My dad at first said no, that I was too young and didn't need to ever worry about shaving my legs. However, he eventually came around to the idea . . . or so I thought.

He and my mom gave me a razor to use, and my mom showed me how she shaved her legs (applying the shaving cream, sitting at the edge of the bathtub, areas to be careful around so I wouldn't cut myself). I used that razor every week to shave my legs, just like my mom had. I used that razor until I was in middle school and actually had leg hair that could be seen. I eventually realized that my leg hair looked just the same after I had "shaved." I asked my parents for a new razor, since mine wasn't working anymore. My dad then admitted to me that the razor he had given me all those years ago had no actual blades in it! He had taken them out. He explained to me that he wanted me to love and honor my body, hair and all. He didn't want me to feel pressured to succumb to others' ideals of what beauty should be. He then went to the store with me to buy a real razor, my mom went over how to use it again, and they gave me the real option of shaving my legs. I definitely started to shave—and continued to through the beginning of high school. But the desire began to fade and eventually I stopped. The confidence my father instilled in me about my own beauty had won. I learned to take pride in things outside of appearance, and I still carry that with me today. Thanks, Dad!

—Brinton, Columbia, SC

Fine, But Don't Stay Out Too Late

When I was a teenager, my parents let me set my own curfew each night I went out. My dad knew that if I got to pick it, I would choose a time that felt late to me (midnight) but wasn't really that late. Plus, he figured I was more likely to stick to it if I picked it. I liked that I got to choose and that it felt like a negotiation that could be tailored to whatever event I was going to rather than a strict rule. **—Kelsey, Salt Lake City, UT**

My brother is four years older than me. When he was in high school and broke curfew or did something wrong, our mom would lecture both of us together because she didn't want to repeat herself in four years. **—Sun-Sun, New York, NY**

When my son, Paul, was sixteen, he was bugging me and my husband about a later curfew. For months we argued, and he got more and more insistent. Finally, we did a little investigation and found that most of his good buddies had a curfew of midnight. One night, we asked him, "What do you want for a curfew?"

He said, "I don't know."

We suggested 12:30 a.m., knowing that most of his friends had to be home by midnight . . . and it was a *big* win! He was never late and, in fact, was home early. He thinks he won, but we really did! **—Regina, Davis, CA**

My parents had an ingenious way of handling our teenage curfews. We would determine the time we should be home after an event, and my parents would set their alarm clock for that time. They would go to sleep at their normal time (long before us teenagers were expected home), and we would quietly go into their room and turn off the alarm when we got home. This way, my parents would sleep through the night without worrying about us but would wake up if we were late. It was very motivating for us and I don't think we were ever late! Although my sister tells of a time when she had to sprint up the stairs and into their room to make it on time.

—Erin, Des Moines, WA

When my daughter (who is now rounding thirty-seven—yikes!) was fourteen, she asked to go to her first concert—Green Day—with a friend at the San Diego Sports Arena. I was adamant that she not go; the fear of weed, drugs, alcohol, and older boys made me crazy! There were tears, and she kept hysterically asking why before she yelled, "You just don't want me to grow up!" Wow—she might as well have thrown ice-cold water in my face. I looked at her and said, "Vanessa, you're right. But I guess that's not an option, is it? I'll check with Janelle's parents to see what the details are as far as driving you and picking you up, and then I will call the Sports Arena Security Office to get some information." That's exactly what I did, and she went to her first concert a happy camper, and nothing bad happened to her! I think this situation helped to solidify the wonderful, open relationship that we have had for the past twenty-plus years. **—Margaret, San Diego, CA**

The first time my daughter asked to go to a party was when she was a sophomore in high school. I asked her if the friend's parents were going to be present. Her reply was "Yes." I said, "Great, I'm going to call them to see if I can drop off some soda and chips." I would always follow through with the phone call, often dropping off some kind of food contribution. I'm sure my daughter figured out that I was ensuring there would be adult supervision, but it was done in a way that didn't embarrass her.

—Kathy, Madison, WI

When I was a preteen, I got in the habit of making plans to sleep over at my friends' houses without running it by my mom first. This was obviously very annoying, and I'm sure would mess up her whole schedule for the day. One day, she had had it. She picked me up after one of these last-minute sleepovers, and instead of yelling at me or grounding me, she promptly drove me to a different friend's house for *another sleepover*. As you may know, after a night away as a kid, you're exhausted and just want the familiarity of your own space and family. She said something along the lines of "Well, since you like hanging out with your friends so much, you can just keep doing it." Even in the moment, I was like, "Damn, she got me on that one." I was miserable and never made a plan without asking again (at least not until I had my own car). **—Rina, Jacksonville, FL**

When I was sixteen, my best friend and I wanted to go to *The Rocky Horror Picture Show* and the cast after-party. It was soooo exciting to have been invited! My mom knew she couldn't tell us no; we would've found some way somehow, even if she forbade it. So she said we could go if we wrote on each other's stomachs in permanent marker: "I'm sixteen and my mom's phone number is xxx-xxxx." With her actual phone number, of course. Then she gave us cab fare and we had a great time at the party! It wasn't as exciting as we thought it was going to be—just a bunch of people sitting around drinking beer and wine and talking. You can bet we kept our shirts on, though. **—Megan, Boston, MA**

We're a Mormon family of six living in the Bay Area. This win has to do with our fabulous sixteen-year-old, makeup-obsessed gay son. Every summer, we've sent our kids to various summer camps at our alma mater, Brigham Young University. Last summer, we wanted our son to attend a weeklong ACT prep camp at BYU because he needed to prepare to take the ACT this fall, and the camp tuition was a great deal less than tutoring here in California.

BYU is extremely conservative and has a strict honor and dress/grooming code, and we knew our son wouldn't be super excited to be around so many other Mormon kids—especially since he wouldn't be able to wear makeup all week. So we bribed him, saying that if he could stay at BYU the entire time, makeup-free, without getting sent home, we would buy him tickets to the (family-friendly) drag show he'd been really wanting to go to. He wanted to go to this show so desperately that he agreed and, despite some early anti-LGBT comments from other campers, he stayed the entire week, received one of the top scores on the ACT test they took the final day of camp—and even ended up becoming friends with the initial instigators. He *loved* the drag show in San Francisco last month. I call that knowing what incentives work for your kid and making the most of the situation!

—**Wendy, Danville, CA**

If You Roll Your Eyes at Me One More Time . . .

When I was in middle school, I was embarrassed to be seen with my parents and so would always walk ten paces behind them. Once, in the mall parking lot, my dad said if I didn't walk next to him, he'd dance like a ballerina. I thought he was bluffing and just rolled my eyes, but then he began pirouetting and leaping around the parking lot. I was mortified and begged him to stop, promising even to hold his hand if I had to! The next week, he was picking me up at school and I was lagging behind him. He mouthed, "Ballet!" and I immediately rushed to his side.

Now, as an adult, I love my dad's humor and humility. And there's no one in the world I'd rather walk with.

—**Kate, Hopkinton, MA**

The first time my daughter rolled her eyes at me, she was about eleven or twelve. My first reaction went something like this:

Me (in my best angry voice): Did you just roll your eyes at me?!

Daughter: [rolls eyes again]

Me: If you are going to roll your eyes at me, then you better start practicing because that one sucked!

Daughter: [has a look of complete confusion on her face]

Me: Now try it like this. [I roll my eyes while sneering and flickering my eyelids.]

Daughter: [attempts to do the same]

Me: No, no, you need to flicker your eyelids. Now do it again! If you're going to roll your eyes at your mother, it has to be good!

This goes on for a good fifteen minutes and ends in total hysterics! She's laughing, I'm laughing, and in the end, my daughter realizes that she doesn't have a typical mom. After that, if she rolls her eyes, it's as a joke, and we head off the dreaded mom-says-black, kid-says-white relationship that characterizes most parent-teen relationships.

—**Damian, Bay Shore, NY**

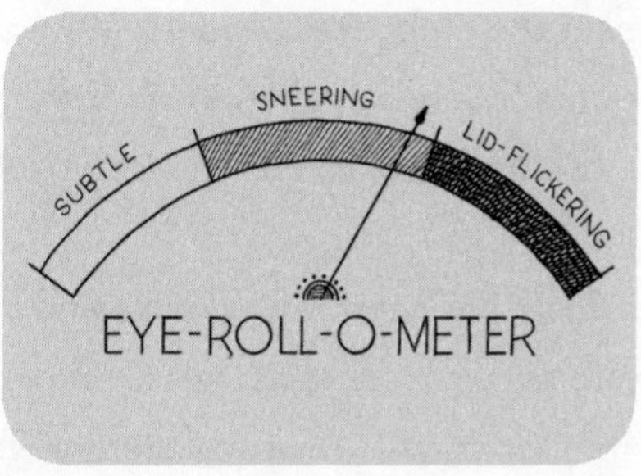

At age seven, my son started complaining that I embarrassed him. I offered him a deal: He could choose one full year when I would not embarrass him in public, but that's all he got. He is eleven now, and every year on his birthday, he has said, "This year." Every year, my husband and I say, "Trust us, you're going to want it later." He hasn't used it yet.

—**Jemma, Lexington, VA**

My daughter, Hannah, was in the fifth grade. At the time, it was teenage fashion to wear low-rise jeans. They were low in the front and the back. Hannah had a habit of pulling them down to make sure they were low and this, inevitably, showed her butt crack. One day, after telling her not to do this many times, we were walking through the schoolyard when she pulled her pants down again. So I cheerfully said, "That's a really good look. I think I'll do the same." I proceeded to pull my pants down to reveal my butt crack and said, "Every time you do it, I'll do it, too." She was horrified, pulled her pants back up, and never did it again. At least not around me.

—Rachel, Walnut Creek, CA

I grew up in the '90s in a blended family household filled with biological and stepsiblings as well as the friends that perpetually spent the night/week/month. With an age spread of only three years among all the siblings, you can image the chaos that dwelled in our modest 1,500-square-foot home.

My mother, bless her heart, was a fierce and consistent disciplinarian. Here are a couple of her wisest moves:

One year for Christmas, when my brother was seventeen, my mother kindly bought him a new battery for his car. He was stoked about the unusually costly gift. My brother quickly learned the downside. After a heated fight, my mother *took away* his car. My brother immediately shot back, "You CAN'T, I bought it! The title is in my name! See ya!" He ran out the front door and to his car. We swiftly heard my brother cursing from outside. My mother slyly shouted out to the driveway, "You may have bought the car, but I bought the battery. The battery has been taken away. You'll have to earn it back." Mom: 1. Teenagers: 0.

In our early adolescent years, door-slamming was a common occurrence in our home. My mother grew tired of the blatant disrespect. After many failed warnings, we came home one day to find our bedroom doors had been replaced with a curtain on a tension rod in our door frames. "You can't slam a curtain, can you?" she cheerfully boasted. Mom: 2. Teenagers: 0.

It didn't take long for my older brother to find his door stowed in the shed. He smartly rehung his bedroom door. My mother looked on with a dangerous smirk. The next morning, my brother awoke to no door and no curtain. My mom had removed his door and driven it an hour north to my grandparents' home. My mother would chirp, "Privacy is a privilege." My brother had to change in the bathroom for the next month until he earned his door back. My siblings and I learned from his mistake and went on to appreciate our curtains. Mom: 3. Teenagers: 0.

Despite my mom's seemingly severe consequences, she was able to work full-time while raising a half-dozen teenagers. We've each grown into respectful, successful adults and are trying our best to pass on those same values to our own kiddos.

—RACHEL, MARSHALL, WI

It's Time You Start Taking Care of Yourself . . . and Me!

My son was in eighth grade. There was a novel required for a class and he absolutely did not want to read it. Much arguing and drama ensued. I found an audio version of the book, and then I yelled at him: "You go down in the basement right now and play Nintendo! Turn off the sound and start listening to this book!" It worked!

This boy was a multitasker, and now he is a well-paid adult who writes computer code while listening to podcasts.

—Kate, Lyons, CO

I hated always having to be the nag. "Pick up your shirt." "Put your books away." "Don't leave that on the steps, take it upstairs." "Flush the toilet when you're done." "Turn your laundry right side out." "Did you miss the bus again?" "Did you forget your track clothes again?"

So I devised several strategies to take the responsibility away from me and put it on the kids.

For items left around the house, I'd make one or two requests in a normal voice. Then I'd pick up the items and put them in my room. If the child wanted them back, they paid a fine (appropriate amount based on allowance and age). The money went to the tzedakah (charity) pot.

For anything that caused me to make an extra trip to school, the kids had to pay into the tzedakah pot for "Mom's taxi." There was always a grace period at the beginning of a school year until we all got into a routine.

All rules applied equally to kids and adults. The plan was that twice a year, we would sit down together as a family to decide what charity would receive the tzedakah fines. The philosophy was that we all had nice things and a nice home. If we didn't appreciate them and wouldn't take care of them, at least those who had less could benefit from our lack of appreciation.

After the first year, there wasn't much in the tzedakah pot and I was no longer the family nag. **—Becky, Delmar, NY**

When I was sixteen, I was taking a course ahead of my year in summer school. Since we lived in a small town with no high school at the time, I was bused during the regular school year. But I spent that summer semester learning how to drive, nervously fumbling my way back and forth to the high school, always under the speed limit. I was afraid to drive, but my mom insisted I needed to learn—she has MS and sometimes her fatigue means she needs my help with driving and errands and such. I thought at the time that was the only thing she was teaching me that summer—but as it turned out, there were a few more adulting lessons up her sleeve.

I've always struggled with social anxiety, and the idea of taking public transit with strangers was a pretty big hurdle. But there were some afternoons that summer when she couldn't pick me up from school—or maybe she wouldn't, I don't know—and busing needed to be done. It happened slowly at first. One day she researched the route, gave me the change I needed, and told me what stop I wanted at what time. I remember being so nervous my first time riding the bus home that summer—I had my headphones on and my nose in a book so no one would try to talk to me. I am still to this day wary of strangers striking up small talk with me on the bus.

As the summer went on, I had to ride the bus a bit more frequently, as there were more and more afternoons my mom "wasn't available." It became less daunting. At the same time, I had to start calling to book my own appointments and other small tasks that seemed annoying at the time. But I think my mom's weird parenting win is the fact that she had (has) this incredibly anxious, stubborn child who needed a gentle hand when it came to being taught how to be an adult. And my mom did that slowly throughout that summer and the time after without my even realizing. Now I'm at university and I ride the bus every day, I make all my own appointments, and I've even traveled to Europe by myself. I still seek treatment for my social anxiety, but my mom gave me the skills I needed to function as an adult, even when I'm anxious, just by doing small things like not picking me up. And I'm really grateful.

—**Christine, Waterloo, ON, Canada**

Growing up, we would take long car trips a couple times a year. To prevent the are-we-there-yet whining, my mom would make copies of the route on maps for my sister and me. At certain map points, we could open a small surprise—but only if we figured out that we had reached the point from map reading. As adults, my sis and I are crazy good at highway navigation. I have also had lots of opportunities to live overseas and I'm crazy good at reading public transportation maps even when I don't understand the language. —**Stephanie, Fort Riley, KS**

When my cousin (now in his early forties) was a teenager, his chore was to take out the trash. He regularly refused to do it, and it often became a fight between my aunt and my cousin. One time, weeks went by, and the trash piled up. All of the regular barrels and yard waste barrels outside were full of trash. He would not take them to the curb on trash day. I was around twelve at the time and happened to be over the night before trash pickup on the fourth week of this. My cousin was out with

friends somewhere, and my aunt asked for my help bringing every last bag of trash out of the barrels and into his bedroom. We spent a great deal of time on this unpleasant task, and by the time we were finished, there were trash bags filling his room, including on his bed. I'm not one to laugh at others' misfortunes, but my aunt is one of the most compassionate, patient, and soft-spoken people I know, so when she had been pushed to her limit, I knew it was serious and I didn't mind helping set my cousin straight. Needless to say, when he got home at whatever hour, he took out the trash.

—**Katie, Amherst, MA**

To avoid cranky teenagers glued to video games and lolling around the house over school breaks, we offer our three teen boys the opportunity to earn video game time up to twice the amount of time they work out. Go for a thirty-minute run, earn an hour of time on video games. Lift weights at the gym for an hour, enjoy two hours battling aliens online. It improves everyone's mood by 100 percent! —**Cherri, Willowbrook, IL**

I'm teaching my kids how the world works through taxes. They get candy? I get a piece for the candy tax. They get string cheese? I take a bite for the cheese tax. And so on and so forth.

Last week, I was in a public restroom with my three-year-old and I got some soap, then swiped some on her hand and used the rest for myself. She said, "Oh, of course! The soap tax!"

I guess it's working! —**Christine, Presque Isle, WI**

My six-year-old has recently been enamored of advertising for certain products—computer programs, toys that I would never buy—and was coming at me with all these pitches she'd heard in commercials. "But moms love this thing!" she'd say. "It's fun and educational, and everybody has one. You have to get it for me!" When I asked where she'd heard all this, she said something along the lines of "Well, everybody knows this, duh." But eventually we sorted out that she'd seen a very convincing ad on the airplane we just took, or on a flyer she brought home from school, and so forth.

"No," I said. "I am not buying that." I explained that it's someone's job to make these things sound great to make you want to buy them—and that they could make a used piece of gum seem great, just by using language and video in an exciting way. She was not convinced, so I grabbed my phone and suggested we start making our own ads for dumb things around the house. For a sweater with huge moth holes in it. For a dried-up purple marker. For getting so dizzy from spinning around in circles that you'd feel kind of sick. It wound up being a hilarious way to harness that wacky kid energy and make some silly home movies, and now when she sees an ad, she'll point out what the advertisers are doing to get us to buy their products! Not that she doesn't still want me to buy stuff, but with a more critical eye she knows when she's being marketed to and can make her own decisions. **—Christa, Chicago, IL**

My parents allotted us two "mental health" days per quarter during our high school years. Basically, they were days we could choose to stay home from school if we needed a break.

This accomplished two things: It allowed us to choose the days and, in a sense, budget our own time off much like an adult; it also, in an indirect way, opened up communication between parent and teen. Rather than faking sick or skipping school, we could be open about needing a break from high school stress.

—**Cara, Massachusetts**

As a parent, I don't believe in giving allowance for doing chores. I really believe that cleaning up after yourself and helping out around the house is part of being in a family and how you contribute to family life, not a job. And while it's appreciated, it's not a means to get paid. But as my son grew older, I knew that he needed to find a way to earn some pocket money (especially because he wanted to buy ingredients for his cooking), so I came up with a scheme where he could earn up to £10 per week based on a series of tasks such as:

- Read an article in today's newspaper/magazine: 50 pence—but if you bring it up for discussion at the dinner table, that bumps it up to £1.
- Write a letter of gratitude to someone who showed you kindness: £1.
- If he could list all the farms his vegetables came from, that was worth £2.

Every week he'd get a list of tasks, and it was up to him if he wanted to earn 50 pence or £10. After a while, these little tasks just became part of his everyday life and he stopped seeking the payment! —**Kara, London, England**

We celebrate our nearly thirteen-year-old child's increasing maturity and capability each birthday by adding a new household responsibility each year—along with the choice of a present, a weekend trip, or a party. We sell this to him as a way to build trust between us, teach him to take responsibility, and give him the skills to feel ready to live on his own when he goes to college—and he is invested in this ideology.

At five, he retrieved the mail from the mailbox. In kindergarten, he began making his lunch for school. First grade brought the tasks of emptying the dishwasher and putting the dishes away. The ways we can count on him continued to grow: trash duty, doing his own laundry, cooking a meal a week and his own brunch on the weekends, mowing the yard, and helping to clean our home and Grandma's house. On vacations, he tracks all receipts in our family budget book, and he now has concocted a ledger system for allocating his allowance, too.

He also speaks easily to selected strangers, like store employees, because we find such interactions and self-advocacy more valuable than cultivating an irrational fear of all unknown adults.

We quiz him about which routes to take to get places so that he won't be lost or dependent when he drives or ventures out on his own, and we encourage him to take bike rides and jogs around our neighborhood on his own or with a friend.

He seems to be growing into a capable young man who always appreciates what we do for him, so it's working so far!

—Debi, Lake Saint Louis, MO

My two kids are in their twenties. Their dad and I divorced when they were five and two. My daughter, the older one, helped me with her brother—everything from getting his shoes on to helping him pick out his clothes. That is, until the age of four. He always wanted it his way, and when he didn't get what he wanted, he would throw a fit.

Once he was in middle school, we started talking about money. We would go over my paycheck, then bills for that check, and calculate how much was left over after gas, groceries, etc. This was very eye-opening to him, because as a single mom, usually what was left was $200 until the next paycheck. He finally understood that spending $45 on shorts or $100 on shoes just for him would mean we might not have enough to last us until the next paycheck.

This made him very driven to make his own money. When he was fourteen, he started buying and selling Rubik's cubes, then graduated to sneakers. There was a Facebook group for sneakerheads in our city. He would set the meet-up spot at a public place, then I would drive him. He did this for a year and saved up enough money to put a $1,300 down payment on a used car, and I paid the rest of it.

—Russica, Farmer's Branch, TX

At the age of sixteen, I got in my first car accident while rushing home from the grocery store with a can of water chestnuts for an Asian meal I was preparing for myself and my mother.

See, when my brother and I were both young teenagers, my mother got frustrated with the volume of food we were eating. Unable to keep up with our snacking, she decided to split the grocery bill and give us each our equal share of the money and bring us along on the weekly shopping trip.

It turned out we were quite different in our approaches to food. My brother was a bit of an optimizer, obsessing about coupons, and he would stock up on premade meals and frozen dinners to meet our mother's nutrition requirements—then use the leftover funds to buy ice cream and potato chips. I apparently had a desire to take things up a notch, so the first thing I did was to use some of the money to get a subscription to a cooking magazine, which led to me making fancier and more complicated meals. My mother was not an especially great cook, known for burning water and the common log of spaghetti because she forgot to stir the pot after dropping the noodles in. I quickly surpassed my mother's cooking skills, to the point where she was jealous of the meals I was eating. She eventually forfeited her portion of the grocery bill to me so I could cook for her. My brother was too attached to his Pringles to buy in to my methods, but my mom definitely won out by not having to worry about ensuring there was always enough food in the house for us. **—Thomas, Edinburgh, Scotland**

When I was fourteen or so, I kept hassling my mum to take me traveling. I had never left the country and desperately wanted to explore the world. Money was tight in my household, and my single mother laughed me off and said, "If you want to go on vacation, you'd better get a job!"

So I found a job bagging groceries at the local supermarket. After a year, I'd saved up a few thousand dollars and went back to my mum to tell her I was ready! She made me write up a report about each of the five places I was most interested in visiting and why. That spring we spent three weeks in Turkey and

Greece—she made me plan most of the trip. We traveled cheaply, but it was an amazing experience. I learned about working, saving money, travel planning, budgeting, and got to visit the Mediterranean all by the time I was fifteen! Looking back, that was a massive parenting win on her part.

—Emily, Montreal, QC, Canada

I left it to my dad to start teaching my teenage daughter to drive. We live in a sprawling metro area, without a lot of good public transit options, so I knew it was really important for my daughter to learn to drive. But the thought of her behind the wheel has terrified me from the time she was little. She's a bit of a daydreamer and has never really paid attention to locations as we've driven her around the city. So when she and her younger sister went out to stay with my parents in western Kansas this summer, I asked my dad if he would at least get her used to the basic operation of a car, along with the rules of the road. He was happy to do it. He took her out driving in his old pickup, so there was no fear of her damaging a nicer, newer car. When I returned to pick up the girls a week later, I got to go for a ride with our family's newest driver. I sat white-knuckled in the back, trying not to say much, while my dad gently coached and encouraged my daughter up front. That was perfect. There were definitely a few moments when I would not have been able to remain as calm as Dad did. I guess that's the beauty of grandparents. Not only have they seen and done it all before—they also have a lower-key relationship with their grandkids that can make teaching them easier.

—Keely, Overland Park, KS

My son really wanted to graduate to the front seat of the car. He was big enough, so I told him if he was old enough to sit up front, he was old enough to take on the responsibility of doing his own laundry. He rode in the front seat while we drove to buy him his own hamper, and he owned the chore from that day forward. When he went away to college, he called to thank me because he couldn't believe how many other freshmen didn't have the first clue how to wash their clothes.

—Hollie, Sacramento, CA

My parents had us sign a driving contract. They printed up an entire contract that detailed their rules for us driving their car while we lived at home or until we got our own car. This contract included things like how much rent we would pay to drive their car each month, how many other kids could ride with us in the car depending on how old we were at the time, and what the consequences would be if we received any kind of ticket or got in an accident that was our fault (on top of law enforcement consequences). If we wanted to drive the car, we had to agree to the contract and sign. I remember feeling a little frustrated about all the extra rules my friends didn't have, but I also remember the responsibility of driving really sinking in. I think it was an awesome way that my parents created some boundaries and put some weight behind the seriousness of driving.

—Lauren, Commerce, MI

I have a son in college, and his first spring break home was hard. I wanted to give him freedom and didn't really set limits, but asked him to be respectful. It didn't go well. He was coming and going at all hours, having loud friends over, and the house was a disaster. I was angry and resentful and felt he was taking advantage of the family.

I was really stressing over how summer break was going to go, when someone suggested that I make a roommate contract with him. So my husband and I sat down and wrote the things that we expected to happen while he was home. These were things like when friends could and couldn't come over, what chores he was expected to do, and general communication expectations, as well as any consequences. Then we asked him what things he needed from us to have the freedom he needed. Finally, we came together and negotiated. If he thought something was unreasonable, it was up for debate and discussion and we all took part in creating the final agreement. This allowed him to feel like we weren't just laying down rules but working together to create a better living situation that we could all be happy with. **—Kendra, Westerville, OH**

Chapter 12

The Art of Manipulating Your Parent

Because once it comes full circle, you have truly won

ONE MORNING WHEN I was in middle school, my dad came into my room after my alarm went off. "Hey, it's a snow day!" he said. "You can go back to sleep."

I was ecstatic.

For about ten seconds. At which point he came back and said, "April Fool's."

Turned out it was just a regular old spring day. And the horror show that is middle school was playing as scheduled.

I'm not sure if that experience, combined with other little tricks my parents had played on me, led me to become a master of elaborate ruses, but become one I did.

It started small—with the Bloody Fairy and my twin sister, Leslie. After Leslie mysteriously disappeared from our house, I moved on to hoaxing my friends. I had my first boyfriend completely convinced that girls didn't fart.

Later, in college, I pulled off what I consider to be my April

Fool's Masterpiece. In 1995, I was living in an artsy co-op with fifteen other students. There was a pay phone on the first floor, and someone had figured out how to cheat the phone so you wouldn't have to pay. On April 1, I sat with a friend, scheming about what might make a fun April Fool's joke on our housemates. Free long-distance calls were all the rage in the house—people giggling and gloating after spending an hour talking to a pal in Texas, a girlfriend in California—and suddenly we realized what we had to do. We had to convince them they'd been caught.

There were a couple of engineering guys we knew who lived in a dorm nearby. We went to their room and filled them in on our evil plot. We'd need someone to call the pay phone and pretend to be a cop. It was too risky, though, for it to be one of them—our housemates knew their voices. So they offered up their friend Stan, who was pre-law. Stan was the kind of guy who, at twenty, already sounded lawyer-ish when just sitting in the cafeteria, complaining about whatever gross thing was for lunch that day. And so when Stan called the pay phone and read the script he'd written, saying that he was Officer Such and Such and that he'd gotten a tip that this phone was being used illegally, nobody questioned his veracity.

By the time my friend and I were back at the co-op, our housemates were in crisis mode. A mandatory meeting had been called, with people gathering in the stairwell because they were too freaked out to even make it to the common room. What was our story gonna be? We all had to tell the same story. We couldn't let anyone get in trouble for this.

At first, I was like, *Holy shit, I can't believe this worked!* And then I was like, *Holy shit, I can't. Believe. This. Worked.* Maybe too well. My conspiratorial friend and I exchanged knowing glances, making a silent pact that we would never tell our housemates the truth. It was clearly too late; they would've skewered us.

For anyone who was on the receiving end of this joke and never figured it out, uh . . . April Fool's! But also, keep reading. What I say next might make you feel better.

Eight years after the pay phone incident, I was working in an after-school program run by the city of Chicago. Three days a week, for three hours each day, I co-taught a class on documentary writing and photography to a group of inner-city high schoolers. We met in one of the science rooms, and the kids sat in pairs in two parallel rows of slab-top tables, preparing autobiographical essays and slideshows that they'd perform at a café at the end of the semester. The program was really cool—the kids weren't called students; they were apprentices. Best of all, they earned an hourly wage.

I loved working with teenagers—I loved their goofiness, their earnestness. I loved helping to draw difficult personal stories out of them with games. So I guess I figured they'd find a little April Fool's joke to be fun. Actually, I didn't really think it through.

It was payday—but at the beginning of class I announced that the checks hadn't come in. I knew it was disappointing, but we'd get it all settled up next week.

The kids were more than disappointed; they were incensed. Couldn't anything be done? Weren't we gonna stick up for them?

We had tried our best, I said. But we were dealing with Chicago bureaucracy and there wasn't a lot we could do. I tried to move on with the writing prompt of the day, but they kept on badgering me with the questions. Finally, I came clean. "April Fool's!" I said, pulling a few of the checks out of my bag and waving them in the air with a gotcha grin.

They all groaned, and we went back to business as usual.

Then, a few minutes later, from the back of the room, a phone rang. This was 2003, pre-smartphones—just a regular old cell phone. We had a silence-your-phone rule, so I figured whoever's phone this was, they'd turn it off. But nope. She picked up.

I was about to tell this apprentice she needed to hang up or take the call from the hallway, when she let out a shriek. "Noooo!" she wailed.

Was it a family death? An illness? An arrest?

"The Sears Tower!" she screamed, leaping out of her seat. "A plane hit the Sears Tower!"

After the Twin Towers fell, Sears (now Willis Tower) became the tallest building in America, and Chicagoans openly wondered if it could be the next target. This was just a year and a half after September 11, and I, like a lot of people, had been living in fear of another terrorist attack. For most of that time, I had refused to fly, traveling back east by train or car.

The girl was now writhing in the aisle in the center of the room, holding her head in her hands and crying. It felt like everyone in the room made a simultaneous gasp.

My co-teacher and I hadn't been trained to handle a situation like this. Why hadn't they trained us?! What were we supposed to do?

But before we could answer that question, the girl rose, walked toward me down the aisle, and slowly lifted her face. Hey eyes had a satisfied glow.

"April Fool's!" she shouted.

And that, my friends, is when I stopped playing tricks on people. I sometimes think about playing them on my daughter. But then I imagine her getting older and outsmarting me just like Sears Tower girl. At least that's what I tell myself it's about.

It could also be, I'm a mom. And I'm just too damn tired.

Weird Kid Wins

When my two brothers and I used to fight (like cats and dogs), my mother used to make us sit in a circle and hold hands. We knew we had to be relatively quiet (at least so my mother couldn't hear us), but we would claw and squeeze the hell out of each other's hands until eventually we'd be laughing and getting along. **—Melissa, Bridgewater, MA**

My four-year-old son came home from school telling me all about a dinosaur game his friend had brought to school. He said he wanted to ask Santa for it. After he was talking about it for a bit, I pulled out my phone and Googled "dinosaur game," and he went through all the pictures with me. Then suddenly he said, "That's it!" And started telling me a fairly elaborate and believable story about how you push the dino's tail down, and use the dice and the tweezers. I made a mental note of it for Christmas, then put him to bed. Later I asked his teacher if this was the game the other boy brought to school. She messaged me back—"What? No, he brought a dinosaur *card* game." My four-year-old had swindled me! When he saw all the options available, he decided to upgrade. **—Heidi, Hillsboro, OR**

My three-and-a-half-year-old has taken to turning the tables and using our parenting phrases on us, which usually amuses us to the point that we end up overlooking what he's trying to get away with. One night when I was trying to tuck him in, he kept playing this god-awful rendition of "Old MacDonald" on a tractor toy. After I told him he absolutely could not press that button again, he did anyway and I could feel my blood pressure rising. But at the conclusion of the song, he cheerfully said, "There, that wasn't so bad, was it?" and I was so caught off guard I didn't know what to say.

—Erin, West Point, NY

My brother is two years older than me, and like any good little sister, I would instigate wrestling matches—but as soon as I lost my edge, I would call out, "Daddy!" And he would come running and finish the wrestling match for me. Weird, I never instigated when my dad wasn't home.

—Katie, Ann Arbor, MI

I was younger than my brother by two years, and when he was old enough, my parents wanted him to start babysitting me. They offered to pay him $2 per hour. He was elated. But I was beyond pissed that he got money for being older. We negotiated a deal. I would get paid, too, 50 cents per hour, but only if they didn't have to resolve a conflict between us when they got home. It worked great. We were both happy and they never came home to a fight! **—Katie, Bellevue, WA**

My mom got a new car that came with two built-in garage-door buttons, one for each side of the two-car garage. This was a fancy new addition to cars back in the '90s. My dad was in the car, attempting to program one side of the garage-door button. My brother and I were standing in the kitchen, holding the garage-door remotes and peeking through the window to the garage so we could see our dad. Whenever he reached up to push the button to open one side, I would push the remote button for the other side so it would also open or close. This went on for a while with our dad scratching his head, wondering why the left door would open when he pushed the right-side button and vice versa. Finally, he came inside and said, "This is driving me nuts. Whenever I push the left side, the right side goes up, too. Whenever I push the right side, the left side goes up, too. I have an electrical engineering degree—I can't believe I can't figure this out!" At that point, my other siblings and my mom (who were also in on the jig) and I lost it and revealed what we were doing. **—Kevin, Wilmington, NC**

I was born in 2001, so I grew up with the Internet. When I was thirteen, my parents caught me watching *Grey's Anatomy* on Netflix and said it was too sexual for me to be watching. I watched it sneakily for a while, creating a secret profile late at night that I would delete before the morning came. That became too cumbersome to do frequently, so I thought that if I watched something "worse" than *Grey's Anatomy,* my parents might change their minds. I picked *Orange Is the New Black* and waited for someone to fall into my trap. My dad saw me watching it and was a little frustrated with my choice, and said I knew that it was inappropriate. I asked him, if I couldn't watch *Orange Is the New Black,* could I at least watch *Grey's Anatomy*? There's nowhere near as much sex in that! He actually granted me permission. I couldn't believe it; I thought I would need to argue. **—River, Portland, OR**

My mom was a single mom, and my brother really gave her a run for her money. At one point when he was in high school, he broke a rule and my mom tried to punish him. She took away his Xbox. Without missing a beat, my brother responded, "Fine. I'm not doing any homework." He shrewdly figured out that my mother cared about his grades much more than he did. And that's when my mom started paying my brother for grades.

—Katherine, Atlanta, GA

When I was in high school, my mom had a rule that I couldn't go into the city with just a group of girls—we had to have boys with us, too, for safety. So I would just make up boys that I would pretend to be picking up. "Okay, Mom, I'm going to pick up Laura, Sarah, Billy, and Joe!" Billy and Joe did not exist. The best part was that I would also use Billy and Joe as an excuse to be late for curfew. I would call my mom and tell her that I needed an extra half hour because I still had to drive Billy and Joe home and I was running late!

—Rachel, Evanston, IL

When I was sixteen, I really wanted to go on a ski trip with my boyfriend and several other high school friends. As I wasn't allowed to spend the night anywhere with my boyfriend (totally reasonable), or go to parties, or hang out at the houses of friends my parents didn't know if their parents weren't there (or even sometimes if they were), my parents were never going to let me go on the ski trip. I asked anyway, hoping I could talk them into it by informing them it would be a big group and not just my boyfriend and I on a romantic weekend getaway. After they said no, I found out an international school club I was part of was planning a ski trip around the same time, and since a good friend that my parents liked would be going, I retyped the permission slip—using the same format and font in case they caught a glimpse of another copy—and extended the dates by two days and had my parents sign it. I went on the trip, and my friend and I went on to meet up with my boyfriend and our other friends the last two days. I'm thirty-four and I have a great relationship with my parents, and have never told them this story. I would feel kind of terrible if they found out that I'd tricked them, but it also reminds me how desperate I was to have more independence than they gave me, and how restricted I felt being the only one of my friends with such protective parents. **—Amanda, San Francisco, CA**

My father, whom I loved, could be difficult. He had a stock phrase when aggravated: "Listen to me now." To help my kids (about ten and twelve) take him in stride before one visit, we told them to remember Pee-wee Herman. The magic words today are "Listen to me now," so cheer when you hear them. When he said the words, we all cheered. My dad was mystified, and we moved on, smiling. Tension avoided!

—Karin, Lynnfield, MA

When I was in high school, I figured out that our report cards were printed with an ink that was erasable and looked a lot like the mark a soft pencil would make. When my report card arrived each semester, I would always make sure to beat my mom to the mailbox and open my report card when she wasn't around. If I got any C's, I would erase them and turn them into B's. She never found out! **—Stephanie, Brooklyn, NY**

If I ever wanted my mom to clean my room, I'd tell her something I was stressed about, so she'd worry about me and then stress-clean my room. I have done this into adulthood. When my own son was born, my mom was secretly cleaning the cat litter to the point that my husband thought our cat just hadn't been moving stuff through! **—Elizabeth, Harrisburg, PA**

I used to unplug the answering machine (I was a 1980s to 1990s kid) when I knew teachers were supposed to call. I would also leave the phone off the hook from the hours of 3:00 p.m. until around 7:00 p.m.—by that time, I figured, it was too late for them to call. If my mom asked about the phone being off the hook, I would just pretend I'd knocked it off accidentally.

I also once created a permission slip using school letterhead and a copy machine that "required cash" for a field trip. I hung out with my friends for a full fun-filled day using the money. **—Elise, Chicago, IL**

I grew up in a suburban town in eastern Massachusetts, where there wasn't much to do for fun as teenagers. When I was seventeen, I was out one night with a group of girlfriends at our local Friendly's restaurant. At a nearby table sat a small group of guys we knew (and liked). We were all into the punk scene and we enjoyed antagonizing each other for fun. We hurled playful insults back and forth between our groups for an hour as we sipped our coffee, and then left. Outside sat a car that belonged to one of the young men in the group we had been messing with that night. We couldn't resist writing all over his car in bright red lipstick, laughing all the while. As we were finishing up our "job," they came outside and caught us in the act. They started screaming that they were going to "get us" (again, playfully), and we whooped and hollered and jumped into my parents' minivan and sped out of the lot, leaving them in our wake. They proceeded to race after us around town on a high-speed late-night race through the suburban streets—it was exciting and a little scary. Finally, I made a quick turn down a busier street and lost them. Us girls all screamed in victory and slapped high fives as I drove off to bring each of my friends home.

As soon as I dropped off my last friend, a terrible thought hit me: The boys all knew where I lived! I sped home as fast as I could, hoping to circumvent any disaster. Too late. By the time I got home, our other family car was trashed, as was my dad's work car that his company owned. I was seriously screwed. My parents and my brother were asleep inside the house, so I tiptoed back and forth between the house and the cars with cleaning products to wash away the ketchup, toothpaste, ice cream, mustard, and other goo that was covering both cars. The problem was, it was an incredibly cold night, and even in the short time that those things had been on the cars, they had frozen solid. I even tried boiling large pots of water and slowly pouring them on the cars, but it barely made a dent in cleaning the mess. My hands were red and raw as I tried desperately to clean them off in the frigid night. I racked my brain for other ideas, knowing my parents would easily determine that I was somehow responsible.

Suddenly I had an idea: I would trash all the cars immediately surrounding my parents' house so that our cars wouldn't look singled out. I crept back upstairs and gathered items that we had enough of so it wouldn't be noticeable if I used some of them: mayonnaise, shaving cream, ketchup, and the like. I completed my mission and made sure I didn't leave any trace connecting it back to our house, and I went to bed.

The next morning, all of our neighbors were outside scrubbing their cars and complaining to one another about the spree on our street. I had been spared!

It wasn't until this Christmas when my parents were visiting me and my family that I finally fessed up to this incident—my parents had no idea! I had succeeding in manipulating them and keeping it secret for twenty-five years.

—**Charlotte, Northampton, MA**

Acknowledgments

PUTTING THIS BOOK together was an amazing experience. Not only did these wins keep me laughing throughout the workday, they changed my parenting. I feel less stuck. Less frustrated. Less like I'm doing it wrong. Because I know that when I'm in conflict with my kid, I can summon my Weird Parenting Tool Kit. I can get instant help from a dad on the other side of the country, a mom on the other side of the globe. Hundreds of people who generously let me—and you—in on their most intimate parenting moments.

One night at dinner, after reminding my daughter for the umpteenth time to not chew with her mouth open, I stopped myself from nagging and tried the Elbow Point. Which resulted in giggles rather than eye rolls. But even if Sasha had rolled her eyes, I'd be prepared with Eye-Roll Coaching. Or maybe if I was really at my limit, I'd declare it our Unbirthday.

If all else fails, we'll always have the Family Scream.

I hope the strategies in this book lead to more wins for you, too. I hope they help you out of your next parenting rut—or to plan ahead for your child's next developmental stage. (I'm already psyched to break out the Curfew Alarm and the Emergency Family Emoji, provided emojis are still a thing when my daughter gets a phone. Will phones still be a thing then?) And for all of you sleep-deprived new parents who feel like you'll never get your life back: While it may be true that your life will never look the same as it did pre-baby, I hope you at least find some inspiration here on stealing moments of me time and recapturing your sex life.

Huge thanks to the *Longest Shortest Time* community for submitting these wins and for answering every question I've ever asked you with heart, enthusiasm, and humor. Thanks also to everyone who solicited submissions from their own communities, especially *This American Life*, Refinery29, Modern Loss, and the Facebook groups Grown & Flown, Moms in Tech, DairyQueens, and WeAreTeachers. I couldn't have made this book without support from my fabulous podcast staff, past and present: Peter Clowney, Andrea Silenzi, Kristen Clark, Abigail Keel, Joanna Solotaroff—and Jackie Sojico, who helped me plan the book and sort through the nearly one thousand submissions we received.

Thank you to my agent, Andrea Morrison, for seeing potential in a handful of weird wins, and to my editor, Joanna Ng, for encouraging me to include my own stories and illustrations. The Spruceton Inn was the perfect space for me to begin those drawings—I was the only guest, in the dead of winter, and I spoke to nobody other than the bartender for a week. (Er, I promise, it was nothing like *The Shining*.) The drawings turned out to be a great way for me to connect with my daughter. After school, she'd run to my drafting table and ask to see my work. She'd ask to hear the story behind each picture, delighted by the tales of parents creatively manipulating their children. "Oh, that's a good one!" she'd say.

I'm grateful to have a kid who loves absurdity as much as I do. And for my husband, Jonathan Menjivar, whose own parenting wins have saved us many times. (Living room chair at the dining room table! Picnic in the snow!) And, finally, for my parents, Leona and Richard Frank, whose wonderful weirdness made me the weirdo I am today.